This book is the story of Benjamin Franklin, a fabulous man for any country — or
any century. But Franklin was American:
as American as the Revolutionary War that
he helped to win; as the Declaration of
Independence that he helped to frame; as
the pioneer diplomatic effort of a young
State which he carried out; as the native
wit with which he endowed his scientific
discoveries and philosophical commentar-
ies. It is a book of Franklin's writings
which afford the reader a picture of his
career — from printer's devil, at the age
of twelve, to the most renowned of inter-
national personages. With tongue-in-cheek
humor he gave rein to his insatiable curiosity: about electricity; about science;
about etiquette; about people young, old,
high-born and born into slavery. In short,
about everything! He was truly a fabulous
American. It is a book that tells you why.

SEVEN SEAS BOOKS

A Collection of Works by Writers in the English Language

THE FABULOUS AMERICAN

A Benjamin Franklin Almanac

THE
FABULOUS
AMERICAN

A BENJAMIN FRANKLIN ALMANAC

Edited and with an
Introduction by Hilda Lass

SEVEN SEAS PUBLISHERS
BERLIN

SEVEN SEAS BOOKS are published by
SEVEN SEAS PUBLISHERS BERLIN
Berlin W 8 · Glinkastrasse 13–15

Copyright 1964 by Seven Seas Books
published as a Seven Seas Book 1964
Cover Design by Lothar Reher
Printed by BBS Heinz Kapelle Pößneck, V 15/34
License Number 306/106/64
Manufactured in the German Democratic Republic

CONTENTS

My dear, dear Polly: Figure to yourself an old man with gray hair appearing under a marten fur cap, among the powdered heads of Paris. It is this odd figure that salutes you, with handfuls of blessings." So wrote Benjamin Franklin, arch-symbol of the revolt of the new order against the old, to a young friend in 1777. He was seventy-one, and he had thought to have retired long since to follow his scientific pursuits and correspond with his learned friends all over the world. Instead, the fabulous American, one of the greatest men of the eighteenth century, was starting a new and dramatic episode in a political career that spanned more than fifty years. He had been appointed by the American Congress to represent at the court of Louis XVI the cause of the thirteen colonies in their revolutionary war against Great Britain, and his was the delicate task of reaching a treaty of alliance with France.

The Congress could not have chosen better. Franklin was already a legend in Europe. He was one of the five authors of the Declaration of Independence. He had already spent seventeen years in England in an effort to settle peaceably the differences between the colonies and the mother country. He had dramatized the grievances of his own province, Pennsylvania, and of the other colonies in his writings. Laws were made for them and they were heavily taxed by a Parliament beyond the seas in which they had no representation; governors were sent from abroad who could override the decisions of their assemblies; foreign soldiers were stationed on their territory, trial by jury was suspended; offenders were shipped to England for trial; swarms of office holders and informers moved in from Britain; the colonies' trade with other countries was restricted and they were not permitted to manufacture steel, woolens, hats and other goods, but had to import them from Britain at high prices. In short, they were the grievances of all colonies since imperialism began.

Franklin had been instrumental in having taxes levied on the huge estates of the proprietors of Pennsylvania – the petty-dictator sons of the original founder of the colony, William Penn – which until then had been tax exempt. His testimony before the House of Commons in London in 1776 on the Stamp Act (a blow to freedom of the press which placed a tax on all newspapers, pamphlets and handbills as well as on every kind of legal paper) was the most important single influence for its repeal. This had won him acclaim not only at home but among the rising British merchants who realized, as he did, that Britain would lose more in trade through the growing boycott than it would gain in taxes.

Franklin was thus the personal embodiment of the ideas behind the American Revolution, which already had deep roots in France as well: that all men are created equal, that they are endowed with certain unalienable rights, among them life, liberty and the pursuit of happiness; that governments derive their powers from the consent of the governed, and that when a government does not serve these ends it is the right of the people to alter or abolish it. John Adams, a future president of the United States, who was in France with Franklin, wrote: "There was scarcely a peasant or a citizen, a valet de chambre, coachman or footman, a lady's chambermaid or a scullion in a kitchen who was not familiar with (his name) and did not consider him a friend to human kind."

Besides, Franklin was the wizard who had flown a kite and captured lightning and with it the imagination of millions, and whose lightning rods had been erected to protect houses all over America and Europe. He was already known to the scientists of Europe, either in person or through his writings, the first American scientist to gain recognition abroad. Through the American Philosophical Society, of which he was first president, and the Royal

Society of London, of whose executive council he was four times a member, he helped to bring together the best minds of the old world and the new. His writings on electricity, which included the fundamental conclusion that electricity is not created by friction but is present in all matter, had been translated into French, German and Italian. In between his political duties he traveled around England and France, pressing for the election of scientists of the three countries to each other's scientific societies and for scientific exchange.

What kind of man was this whose face appeared on snuff-boxes and rings that sold like hot cakes on the streets of Paris, so that he "durst not do anything that would oblige him to run away, as his phiz would discover him wherever he should venture to show it," as Franklin wrote his daughter? The man who was kissed on both cheeks by the grand old man of the French Revolution, Voltaire, in front of a gathering of philosophers, and who was given a fabulous garden party by the Countess d'Houdetot, at which she sang a song of her own composition in his praise?

The colonies into which Franklin was born (in Boston, on January 17 1706) were primitive and isolated settlements, too busy struggling for survival to think in broad terms about communications, united defense against attack, education and culture. Yet by the time he died in 1790, these provincial-minded colonies had been welded into a state founded on the most advanced democratic principles then known, an example to other struggling nations.

Of all the men who came to the surface of colonial life to advance this process, Franklin best represented the progressive qualities the new world had to offer; tremendous energy, a desire to understand and master the physical world, contempt for titles and rank, firm belief in the common man's ability to govern himself.

In this vast wild country which fell so far short of the old world in comforts and conveniences, there was no time for idle philosophizing, no room for luxury. Industry and frugality were needed, pavements, street lights, hospitals, libraries, colleges. The *Junto* which Franklin organized when he was twenty-two, as a club for the exchange of practical scientific and philosophical ideas, became a network of societies on which Franklin could depend in the projects of which he was so often the moving force. He began life as a printer, and soon was publishing the best newspaper in the colonies, the *Pennsylvania Gazette*. He was responsible for the first subscription library, an idea which took hold and made, he said, "the common tradesmen and farmers (of America) as intelligent as most gentlemen from other countries." From there he went on to regulate the city watchman service, organize the first volunteer fire company; he was responsible for Pennsylvania's first hospital for the poor and for its first institution of higher learning, now the University of Pennsylvania.

His famous *Poor Richard's Almanac,* which he produced for twenty-five years, was the most widely read book in America. It included a wealth of useful information and household hints, and through it he reached almost every American family with his doctrine of honest work and thrift as the way to advancement. Franklin was talking to people who really had to pull themselves up by their own boot straps. Quoted out of their historical context as they are today, his sayings often sound like the platitudes that business men like to hang over their employees' desks ("Remember that time is money . . . Remember that credit is money"). But the editors of anthologies who have made Franklin's "Advice to a Young Tradesman," one of his best known works, almost never quote his attacks on laws protecting privilege and wealth, in support of government directly responsible to the people, against slavery, against low wages, or his unequivocal condemnation of war, which show him to have been one of the most progressive men of his time.

Franklin's scientific thinking, like his political ideas,

were always directed to a practical end. He invented a flexible catheter because his brother John suffered from kidney trouble. He studied the Gulf Stream because as postmaster general of the colonies he was interested in shortening the passage of mail packets from England to America. He invented an open stove for warming rooms, still known as the Franklin stove, because he noticed that "many of the diseases proceeding from colds ... fatal to very great numbers of people, may be ascribed to strong-drawing chimneys, whereby in severe weather a man is scorched before while he is froze behind," and because ordinary fireplaces wasted wood. He found time to correspond with dozens of other scientists about evaporation and hydrodynamics, waterspouts and whirlwinds, smallpox and innoculation, the circulation of the blood, the causes of storms. When his eyes began to fail him, he invented bifocal glasses. Somewhere he found time to learn something about music. In 1762 he designed the first musical invention in America, the "armonica," which he based on the principle of musical glasses. It was a series of half hemispheres of various diameters, strung on a rod and turned by a foot pedal, the performer producing the various tones by striking the rims with his fingers. It had a vogue which lasted nearly half a century, and both Mozart and Beethoven composed for it. Franklin's inventions were soon adopted by others, but he never patented or profited by any of them, for "as we enjoy great advantages from the inventions of others, we should be glad of an opportunity to serve others by any invention of ours; and this we should do freely and generously."

In the years 1748–52, when he did most of his work in electricity, he was also a member of the Pennsylvania Assembly, deeply embroiled as a leader of the popular party in the disputes with the hereditary proprietors of Pennsylvania. In this small pot conflicts brewed in miniature which twenty-five years later were to split the British Empire apart in the Revolution of 1776–83. Here Franklin got the training in debate and negotiation which was to serve him so well when he had to deal with the ministers of great powers.

He believed at first that the differences could be solved by a federal union of the colonies with Britain, with America represented in Parliament and the right to vote on the laws with which it was expected to comply. He argued this position in Britain on behalf of the colonies with passion and logic, until he became convinced that there was no compromising with the King's corrupt and short-sighted ministers. Warm friends among British liberals, whose personal interests as well as their sense of justice put them in violent opposition to the despotic and rotten rule of George III, sympathized with him and with the colonies' grievances.

"The people of England are ... just and generous," Franklin's friend David Hartley, an opposition member of Parliament, wrote him in 1776, "and, if it were put to the sense of the people of England, you would not be left in any doubt whether it was *want of will*, or *want of power*, to do you justice. You know the blot of our constitution, by which, to our disgrace and to your misfortune, a corrupt ministry sheltered by Parliamentary influence are out of our immediate control."

Actually the people of England had expressed themselves much more violently than this in the riots and strikes against unemployment which followed the end of the Seven Years' War with France in 1763, and the strikes and demonstrations in 1768 in favor of the popular leader, John Wilkes, an outspoken supporter of America's cause, who was three times elected to Parliament and each time unseated and exiled, brought England close to civil war. Mass dissatisfaction prevented Britain from throwing her full strength into the war with the colonies. Without the strong opposition to George's rule at home, it is unlikely that America could have won her victory – a victory that was in turn a blow for British Parliamentary democracy.

While the military battles were fought on American soil, diplomatic maneuvers of the most refined sort had to be conducted in France, and it is doubtful whether anyone with less breadth of vision and tact than Franklin could have carried them through with success. The colonies were without money to buy ammunition abroad or pay soldiers at home. Congress had no federal authority to tax. In this situation there was nothing to do but to solicit aid from the country most interested in seeing England defeated. Yet France, as a monarchy, was being asked to help establish a republic which would set an example to her own people. A statistical measure of Franklin's persuasiveness is the fact that he negotiated loans totaling eighteen million pounds at Versailles, often having to beg for money after Congress had already spent it.

The drawn-out negotiations for reaching peace with defeated England were also largely in Franklin's hands. When he finally left France in 1785, covered with honors and carrying a miniature of the king set with 408 diamonds, he was seventy-nine, and so ill with kidney stone that he could hardly travel. Yet he was plunged immediately into American politics as president of his home state of Pennsylvania and as a delegate to the convention that drew up the constitution of the United States. He did not escape public affairs until the day of his death.

Yet if Franklin had done nothing else, he could have won a place in history with his wit and wisdom. These, with his willingness to defer to the opinions of others and to test his own again and again, won him enormous popularity with men and women alike. William Strahan, printer to the King of England, wrote to Mrs. Franklin from London in 1757 in an effort to persuade her to join her husband abroad: "I never saw a man who was, in every respect, so perfectly agreeable to me. Some are amiable in one view, some in another, he in all . . . I know the ladies here consider him in exactly the same light I do (and) upon my word I think you should come over, with all convenient speed, to look after your interest . . . ."

Mrs. Franklin never did – she feared the long sea voyage – and she died in 1775 while Franklin was in England, but all during their long separation they kept up an active correspondence which reflect a busy man's interest in the minutiae of household and family affairs. It also reveals one reason for Franklin's obvious appeal for women: he took them seriously – their small personal problems and their intellectual interests. Some of his most interesting scientific letters, for example, were written to the young daughter of his London landlady, Mary Stevenson, who suggested that they correspond on philosophical subjects. "After writing six folio pages of philosophy to a young girl, is it necessary to finish such a letter with a compliment?" he asks at the end of a highly complex discourse on tides in rivers.

This collection is an attempt to present Franklin the versatile and complex personality who played such an important part in one of the key transition periods of modern history, climaxing in the American and French revolutions. Benjamin Franklin embodied to a singular degree a concept then quite new in the world and still battling for its place today – that of the ordinary man who believes he has the right and the power to change the world, armed with scientific knowledge, common sense, and the understanding that his own interests can best be served by serving society's. At the peak of his fame, Franklin never thought of himself as a man who was pulling the strings of history. When the famous French economist and statesman Turgot coined the classic lines, "He snatched the lightning from the sky and the sceptre from tyrants," Franklin's comment was typical. "It ascribes too much to me," he said, "especially in what relates to the tyrant; the Revolution having been the work of many brave men."

The selections chosen show him as printer, inventor and public-spirited citizen at home, as statesman and philosopher in England and France, as a man of incomparable

15

wit and good humor in his lighter moments, and finally as an elder statesman trying to put into action in the newly established United States the ideals of popular democracy for which so many people on both sides of the ocean had worked and fought. It is impossible to do justice here to his political and scientific writings which fill many volumes.

Two of his best-known pieces have been included – his Conversation with the Gout and the Pro-Slavery Parody – although readers will find them in two other Seven Seas Books collections: Gertrude Gelbin's *Song to Generations* and Herbert Aptheker's *And Why Not Every Man?*, respectively.

Franklin's spelling and punctuation have been modernized for the convenience of the reader.

HILDA LASS

Prague, 1963

PRINTER
AND PUBLIC – SPIRITED CITIZEN

From a child I was fond of reading, and all the little money that came into my hands was ever laid out in books ... This bookish inclination at length determined my father to make me a printer, though he had already one son (James) of that profession. In 1717 my brother James returned from England with a press and letters to set up his business in Boston. I liked it much better than that of my father, but still had a hankering for the sea. To prevent the apprehended effect of such an inclination, my father was impatient to have me bound to my brother. I stood out for some time, but at last was persuaded, and signed the indentures when I was yet but twelve years old. I was to serve as an apprentice till I was twenty-one years of age, only I was to be allowed journeyman's wages during the last year.

In a little time I made great proficiency in the business, and became a useful hand to my brother. I now had access to better books. An acquaintance with the apprentices of booksellers enabled me sometimes to borrow a small one, which I was careful to return soon and clean. Often I sat up in my room reading the greatest part of the night, when the book was borrowed in the evening and to be returned early in the morning, lest it should be missed or wanted ....

There was another bookish lad in the town, John Collins by name, with whom I was intimately acquainted. We sometimes disputed, and very fond we were of argument, and very desirous of confuting one another, which disputatious turn, by the way, is apt to become a very bad habit, making people often very disagreeable in company by the contradiction that is necessary to bring it into practice; and thence, besides souring and spoiling the conversation, is productive of disgusts and, perhaps, enmities where you may have occasion for friendship. I had caught it by reading my father's books of dispute about religion. Persons of good sense, I have since observed, seldom fall into it, except lawyers, university men, and men of all sorts that have been bred at Edinborough.

A question was once, somehow or other, started between Collins and me, of the propriety of educating the female sex in learning, and their abilities for study. He was of opinion that it was improper, and that they were naturally unequal to it. I took the contrary side, perhaps a little for dispute's sake. He was naturally more eloquent, had a ready plenty of words; and sometimes, as I thought, bore me down more by his fluency than by the strength of his reason.

As we parted without settling the point, and were not to see one another again for some time, I sat down to put my arguments in writing, which I copied fair and sent to him. He answered, and I replied. Three or four letters of a side had passed, when my father happened to find my papers and read them. Without entering into the discussion, he took occasion to talk to me about the manner of my writing; observing that, though I had the advantage of my antagonist in correct spelling and pointing (which I owed to the printing-house), I fell far short in elegance of expression, in method and in perspicuity, of which he convinced me by several instances. I saw the justice of his remarks, and thence grew more attentive to the manner in writing, and determined to endeavor at improvement.

About this time I met with an odd volume of the *Spectator**. It was the third. I had never before seen any of them. I bought it, read it over and over, and was much delighted with it. I thought the writing excellent, and wished, if possible, to imitate it. With this view I took some of the papers and, making short hints of the sentiments in each sentence, laid them by a few days, and then, without looking at the book, tried to complete the papers again, by expressing each hinted sentiment at length, and as fully as it had been expressed before, in any suitable

* London daily published 1711–12, notable for the contributions of Joseph Addison and Richard Steele.

words that should come to hand. Then I compared my *Spectator* with the original, discovered some of my faults, and corrected them.

But I found I wanted a stock of words or a readiness in recollecting and using them, which I thought I should have acquired before that time if I had gone on making verses; since the continual occasion for words of the same import, but of different length, to suit the measure, or of different sound for the rhyme, would have laid me under a constant necessity of searching for variety, and also have tended to fix that variety in my mind, and make me master of it. Therefore I took some of the tales and turned them into verse; and, after a time, when I had pretty well forgotten the prose, turned them back again.

I also sometimes jumbled my collections of hints into confusion, and after some weeks endeavored to reduce them into the best order, before I began to form the full sentences and complete the paper. This was to teach method in the arrangement of thoughts. By comparing my work afterwards with the original, I discovered many faults and amended them; but I sometimes had the pleasure of fancying that, in certain particulars of small import, I had been lucky enough to improve the method or the language, and this encouraged me to think I might possibly in time come to be a tolerable English writer, of which I was extremely ambitious . . . .

While I was intent on improving my language, I met with an English grammar (I think it was Greenwood's), at the end of which there were two little sketches of the arts of rhetoric and logic, the latter finishing with a specimen of a dispute in the Socratic method; and soon after I procured Xenophon's *Memorable Things of Socrates,* wherein there are many instances of the same method. I was charmed with it, adopted it, dropt my abrupt contradiction and positive argumentation, and put on the humble inquirer and doubter. And being then, from reading Shaftsbury and Collins, become a real doubter in many

ENTRY INTO PHILADELPHIA

When Franklin was seventeen he broke with his brother, and because he could not get work as a printer in Boston he decided to go to New York. There he was given a recommendation to a Philadelphia printer. He arrived in that city on a Sunday morning after a trip full of mishaps.

I have been the more particular in this description of my journey and shall be so of my first entry into that city, that you may in your mind compare such unlikely beginnings with the figure I have since made there. I was in my working dress, my best clothes being to come round by sea. I was dirty from my journey; my pockets were stuffed out with shirts and stockings, and I knew no soul nor where to look for lodging. I was fatigued with traveling, rowing, and want of rest. I was very hungry, and my whole stock of cash consisted of a Dutch dollar, and about a shilling in copper. The latter I gave the people of the boat for my passage who at first refused it on account of my rowing; but I insisted on their taking it. A man being somewhat more generous when he has but a little money than when he has plenty, perhaps through fear of being thought to have but little.

Then I walked up the street, gazing about till near the market house I met a boy with bread. I had made many a meal on bread, and inquiring where he got it I went immediately to the baker's he directed me to, in Second Street, and asked for a biscuit, intending such as we had in Boston; but they, it seems, were not made in Philadelphia. Then I asked for a three-penny loaf and was told they had none such. So not considering or knowing the difference of money and the greater cheapness nor the names of his bread, I bade him give me three-penny worth of any sort. He gave me, accordingly, three great puffy rolls. I was surprised at the quantity but took it, and having no room in my pockets, walked off with a roll under each arm and eating the other.

Thus I went up Market Street as far as Fourth Street, passing by the door of Mr. Read, my future wife's father; when she, standing at the door, saw me and thought I made, as I certainly did, a most awkward, ridiculous appearance. Then I turned and went down Chestnut Street and part of Walnut Street, eating my roll all the way, and, coming round, found myself again at Market Street wharf, near the boat I came in, to which I went for a draught of the river water; and, being filled with one of my rolls, gave the other two to a woman and her child that came down the river in the boat with us and were waiting to go further.

Thus refreshed, I walked again up the street, which by this time had many clean-dressed people in it, who were all walking the same way. I joined them and thereby was led into the great meeting-house of the Quakers near the market. I sat down among them, and after looking round awhile and hearing nothing said, being very drowsy through labor and want of rest the preceding night, I fell fast asleep, and continued so till the meeting broke up, when one was kind enough to rouse me. This was, therefore, the first house I was in, or slept in, in Philadelphia.

– From the *Autobiography, Part 1*
1771

RULES FOR A CLUB
ESTABLISHED FOR MUTUAL IMPROVEMENT

Franklin in his Autobiography tells how, in 1728, he organized his most "ingenious" friends into a club for mutual improvement called the Junto. *It met every Friday night and each member in turn proposed topics of morals, politics or natural philosophy for discussion. Once in three months each member had to produce and read an essay of his own writing on any subject he chose. The debates were to be "conducted in the sincere spirit of inquiry after truth without fondness for dispute or desire of victory." The twenty-four questions published here were drawn up by Franklin as a guide to discussion.*

Problems debated by the Junto *ranged from "Can any one particular form of government suit all mankind?" to "How may smokey chimneys best be cured?" The original twelve members included three printers besides Franklin, a copyer of deeds, a surveyor, a joiner and a shoemaker. The* Junto *expanded and kept alive for decades, and grew into the American Philosophical Society, with Franklin as its first president, in 1769.*

Have you read over these queries this morning in order to consider what you might have to offer the *Junto* touching any one of them? *viz.*

1. Have you met with anything in the author you last read, remarkable or suitable to be communicated to the *Junto?* particularly in history, morality, poetry, physic, travel, mechanic arts, or other parts of knowledge.

2. What new story have you lately heard agreeable for telling in conversation?

3. Hath any citizen in your knowledge failed in his business lately, and what have you heard of the cause?

4. Have you lately heard of any citizen's thriving well and by what means?

5. Have you lately heard how any present rich man, here or elsewhere, got his estate?

6. Do you know of a fellow citizen who has lately done a worthy action, deserving praise and imitation; or

who has lately committed an error, proper for us to be warned against and avoid?

7. What unhappy effects of intemperance have you lately observed or heard; of imprudence, of passion, or of any other vice or folly?

8. What happy effects of temperance, of prudence, of moderation, or of any other virtue?

9. Have you or any of your acquaintance been lately sick or wounded? If so, what remedies were used and what were their effects?

10. Whom do you know that are shortly going on voyages or journeys, if one should have occasion to send by them?

11. Do you think of anything at present in which the *Junto* may be serviceable to *mankind*, to their country, to their friends, or to themselves?

12. Hath any deserving stranger arrived in town since last meeting, that you have heard of? And what have you heard or observed of his character or merits? And whether, think you, it lies in the power of the *Junto* to oblige him, or encourage him as he deserves?

13. Do you know of any deserving young beginner lately set up, whom it lies in the power of the *Junto* any way to encourage?

14. Have you lately observed any defect in the laws of your *country* of which it would be proper to move the legislature for an amendment? Or do you know of any beneficial law that is wanting?

15. Have you lately observed any encroachment on the just liberties of the people?

16. Hath any body attacked your reputation lately? And what can the *Junto* do towards securing it?

17. Is there any man whose friendship you want and which the *Junto*, or any of them, can procure for you?

18. Have you lately heard any member's character attacked and how have you defended it?

19. Hath any man injured you, from whom it is in the power of the *Junto* to procure redress?

20. In what manner can the *Junto*, or any of them, assist you in any of your honorable designs?

21. Have you any weighty affair on hand in which you think the advice of the *Junto* may be of service?

22. What benefits have you lately received from any man not present?

23. Is there any difficulty in matters of opinion, of justice and injustice which you would gladly have discussed at this time?

24. Do you see anything amiss in the present customs or proceedings of the *Junto* which might be amended?

Any person to be qualified (as a member of the *Junto*) to stand up and lay his hand upon his breast, and be asked these questions, *viz*.

1. Have you any particular disrespect to any present members?
   Answer. I have not.

2. Do you sincerely declare that you love mankind in general, of what profession or religion soever?
   Answer. I do.

3. Do you think any person ought to be harmed in his body, name or goods for mere speculative opinion or his external way of worship?
   Answer. No.

4. Do you love truth for truth's sake, and will you endeavor impartially to find and receive it yourself, and communicate it to others?
Answer. Yes.

A MODEST INQUIRY
INTO THE NATURE AND NECESSITY
OF A PAPER CURRENCY

This was the author's first work of a political nature, published in 1729 when he was twenty-three. There was a strong popular demand in Pennsylvania province for more paper currency to stimulate trade and employment, but the wealthy were against it, fearing it would depreciate. The point had been discussed in Franklin's club, the Junto, *and he had become convinced of the need for a currency issue. His pamphlet, published anonymously, helped this point of view to carry the day.*

In the brief excerpt published here, dealing with commodity exchange and the nature of money, Franklin develops the theory that labor is the measure of value forty-six years before it was formulated by Adam Smith in "The Wealth of Nations." Referring to the essay, Karl Marx speaks of "the celebrated Franklin, one of the first economists, after William Petty, who saw through the nature of value*."

As Providence has so ordered it that not only different countries but even different parts of the same country have their peculiar most suitable productions, and likewise that different men have geniuses adapted to a variety of different arts and manufactures; therefore *commerce,* or the exchange of one commodity or manufacture for another, is highly convenient and beneficial to mankind. As for

* Karl Marx, Vol. I, Modern Library (N. Y., 1936) p. 59

instance, A may be skilful in the art of making cloth and B understand the raising of corn. A wants corn, and B cloth, upon which they make an exchange with each other for as much as each has occasion for, to the mutual advantage and satisfaction of both.

But it would be very tedious if there were no other way of general dealing but by an immediate exchange of commodities; because a man that had corn to dispose of and wanted cloth for it might, perhaps, in his search for a chapman to deal with, meet with twenty people that had cloth to dispose of but wanted no corn; and with twenty others that wanted his corn but had no cloth to suit with; to remedy such inconveniences and facilitate exchange, men have invented **MONEY**, properly called a *medium of exchange,* because through or by its means labor is exchanged for labor, or one commodity for another. And whatever particular thing men have agreed to make this medium of, whether gold, silver, copper or tobacco, it is, to those who possess it (if they want anything) that very thing they want, because it will immediately procure it for them.

It is cloth to him that wants cloth, and corn to those that want corn; and so of all other necessaries it *is* whatsoever it will procure. Thus he who had corn to dispose of and wanted to purchase cloth with it might sell his corn for its value in this general medium to one who wanted corn but had no cloth; and with this medium he might purchase cloth of him that wanted no corn but perhaps some other thing as iron, it may be, which this medium will immediately procure, and so he may be said to have exchanged his cloth for iron; and thus the general change is soon performed, to the satisfaction of all parties, with an abundance of facility.

For many ages those parts of the world which are engaged in commerce have fixed upon gold and silver as the chief and most proper materials for this medium; they being in themselves valuable metals for their fineness, beauty and scarcity. By these, particularly by silver, it has been usual to value all things else. But as silver itself is of no certain permanent value, being worth more or less according to its scarcity or plenty, therefore it seems requisite to fix upon something else, more proper to be made a *measure of values,* and this I take to be labor.

By labor may the value of silver be measured as well as other things. As, suppose one man employed to raise corn, while another is digging and refining silver; at the year's end, or at any other period of time, the complete produce of corn and that of silver are the natural price of each other; and if one be twenty bushels and the other twenty ounces, then an ounce of that silver is worth the labor of raising a bushel of that corn. Now if by the discovery of some nearer, more easy or plentiful mines a man may get forty ounces of silver as easily as formerly he did twenty, and the same labor is still required to raise twenty bushels of corn, then two ounces of silver will be worth no more than the same labor of raising one bushel of corn, and that bushel of corn will be as cheap at two ounces as it was before at one. . . .

A PLAN FOR ACHIEVING MORAL PERFECTION

It was about this time [1730] I conceived the bold and arduous project of arriving at moral perfection. I wish'd to live without committing any fault at any time; I would conquer all that either natural inclination, custom, or company might lead me into. As I knew, or thought I knew, what was right and wrong, I did not see why I might not always do the one and avoid the other. But I soon found I had undertaken a task of more difficulty than I had imagined. While my care was employ'd in guarding against one fault, I was often surprised by another; habit took the advantage of inattention; inclination was sometimes too strong for reason. I concluded, at length, that the mere speculative conviction that it was our interest to be completely virtuous, was not sufficient to prevent our slipping; and that the contrary habits must be broken, and good ones acquired and established, before we can have any dependence on a steady, uniform rectitude of conduct. For this purpose I therefore contrived the following method.

In the various enumerations of the moral virtues I had met with in my reading, I found the catalogue more or less numerous, as different writers included more or fewer ideas under the same name. Temperance, for example, was by some confined to eating and drinking, while by others it was extended to mean the moderating every other pleasure, appetite, inclination, or passion, bodily or mental, even to our avarice and ambition. I propos'd to myself, for the sake of clearness, to use rather more names, with fewer ideas annex'd to each, than a few names with more ideas; and I included under thirteen names of virtues all that at that time occurr'd to me as necessary or desirable, and annexed to each a short precept, which fully express'd the extent I gave to its meaning.

These names of virtues, with their precepts, were:

TEMPERANCE   Eat not to dullness, drink not to elevation.

SILENCE   Speak not but what may benefit others or yourself; avoid trifling conversation.

ORDER   Let all your things have their places; let each part of your business have its time.

RESOLUTION   Resolve to perform what you ought; perform without fail what you resolve.

FRUGALITY   Make no expense but to do good to others or yourself; i. e., waste nothing.

INDUSTRY   Lose no time; be always employ'd in something useful; cut off all unnecessary actions.

SINCERITY   Use no hurtful deceit; think innocently and justly; and, if you speak, speak accordingly.

JUSTICE   Wrong none by doing injuries, or omitting the benefits that are your duty.

MODERATION   Avoid extremes; forbear resenting injuries so much as you think they deserve.

CLEANLINESS   Tolerate no uncleanliness in body, clothes, or habitation.

TRANQUILLITY   Be not disturbed at trifles, or at accidents common or unavoidable.

CHASTITY   Rarely use venery but for health or offspring, never to dullness, weakness, or the injury of your own or another's peace or reputation.

HUMILITY   Imitate Jesus and Socrates.

My intention being to acquire the *habitude* of all these virtues, I judg'd it would be well not to distract my attention by attempting the whole at once, but to fix it on one of them at a time; and, when I should be master of that, then to proceed to another, and so on, till I should have gone through the thirteen; and, as the previous acquisition of some might facilitate the acquisition of certain others, I arrang'd them with that view, as they stand above.

Temperance first, as it tends to procure that coolness and clearness of head, which is so necessary where constant vigilance was to be kept up, and guard maintained against the unremitting attraction of ancient habits, and the force of perpetual temptations. This being acquir'd and established, *Silence* would be more easy; and my desire being to gain knowledge at the same time that I improv'd in virtue, and considering that in conversation it was obtain'd rather by the use of the ears than of the tongue, and therefore wishing to break a habit I was getting into of prattling, punning, and joking, which only made acceptable to trifling company, I gave *Silence* the second place.

This and the next, *Order,* I expected would allow me more time for attending to my project and my studies. *Resolution,* once become habitual, would keep me firm in my endeavors to obtain all the subsequent virtues; *Frugality* and *Industry* freeing me from my remaining debt, and producing affluence and independence, would make more easy the practice of *Sincerity* and *Justice,* etc., etc. Conceiving then, that, agreeably to the advice of Pythagoras in his Golden Verses, daily examination would be necessary, I contrived the following method for conducting that examination.

I made a little book, in which I allotted a page for each of the virtues. I rul'd each page with red ink, so as to have seven columns, one for each day of the week, marking each column with a letter of the day. I cross'd these columns with thirteen red lines, marking the beginning of each line with the first letter of one of the ʳtues, on which line, and in its proper column, I might mai̇ by a little black spot, every fault I found upon examination have been committed respecting that virtue upon that day....

I enter'd upon the execution of this plan for self-examination, and continu'd it with occasional intermissions for some time. I was surpris'd to find myself so much fuller of faults than I had imagined; but I had the satisfaction of seeing them diminish. To avoid the trouble of renewing now and then my little book, which, by scraping out the marks on the paper of old faults to make room for new ones in a new course, became full of holes, I transferr'd my tables and precepts to the ivory leaves of a memorandum book, on which the lines were drawn with red ink, that made a durable stain, and on those lines I mark'd my faults with a black-lead pencil, which marks I could easily wipe out with a wet sponge. After a while I went through one course only in a year, and afterward only one in several years, till at length I omitted them entirely, being employ'd in voyages and business abroad, with a multiplicity of affairs that interfered; but I always carried my little book with me.

My scheme of ORDER gave me the most trouble; and I found that, though it might be practicable where a man's business was such as to leave him the disposition of his time, that of a journeyman printer, for instance, it was not possible to be exactly observed by a master, who must mix with the world, and often receive people of business at their own hours. *Order,* too, with regard to places for things, papers, etc. I found extremely difficult to acquire. I had not been early accustomed to it, and having an exceeding good memory, I was not so sensible of the inconvenience attending want of method.

This article, therefore, cost me so much painful attention, and my faults in it vexed me so much, and I made so little progress in amendment, and had such frequent relapses, that I was almost ready to give up the attempt, and content myself with a faulty character in that respect, like the man who, in buying an axe of a smith, my neighbor, desired to have the whole of its surface as bright as the edge. The smith consented to grind it bright for him if he would turn the wheel; he turn'd, while the smith press'd the broad face of the axe hard and heavily on the stone, which made the turning of it very fatiguing. The man came every now and then from the wheel to see how the work went on, and at length would take his axe as it was, without farther grinding.

"No," said the smith, "turn on, turn on; we shall have it bright by-and-by; as yet, it is only speckled."

"Yes," says the man, *"but I think I like a speckled axe best."*

And I believe this may have been the case with many, who, having, for want of some such means as I employ'd, found the difficulty of obtaining good and breaking bad habits in other points of vice and virtue, have given up the struggle, and concluded that *"a speckled axe was best";* for something, that pretended to be reason, was every now and then suggesting to me that such extreme nicety as I exacted of myself might be a kind of foppery in morals, which, if it were known, would make me ridiculous; that a perfect character might be attended with the inconvenience of being envied and hated; and that a benevolent man should allow a few faults in himself, to keep his friends in countenance....

– From the *Autobiography, Part II*
1784

A PRINTER'S PHILOSOPHY

Being frequently censured and condemned by different persons for printing things which they say ought not to be printed, I have sometimes thought it might be necessary to make a standing apology for myself, and publish it once a year, to be read upon all occasions of that nature. Much business has hitherto hindered the execution of this design; but, having very lately given extraordinary offence by printing an advertisement with a certain N. B. at the end of it, I find an apology more particularly requisite at this juncture, though it happens when I have not yet leisure to write such a thing in the proper form, and can only in a loose manner throw those considerations together which should have been the substance of it.

I request all who are angry with me on the account of printing things they don't like, calmly to consider these following particulars:

1. That the opinions of men are almost as various as their faces: an observation general enough to become a common proverb: *So many men so many minds.*

2. That the business of printing has chiefly to do with men's opinions; most things that are printed tending to promote some, or oppose others.

3. That hence arises the peculiar unhappiness of that business, which other callings are no way liable to; they who follow printing being scarce able to do anything in their way of getting a living, which shall not probably give offence to some and perhaps to many; whereas the smith, the shoemaker, the carpenter, or the man of any other trade may work indifferently for people of all persuasions without offending any of them; and the merchant may buy and sell with Jews, Turks, heretics, and infidels of all sorts, and get money by every one of them, without giving offence to the most orthodox, of any sort; or suffering the least censure or ill-will on the account from any man whatever.

4. That it is as unreasonable in any one man or set of men to expect to be pleased with everything that is printed, as to think that nobody ought to be pleased but themselves.

5. Printers are educated in the belief that when men differ in opinion both sides ought equally to have the advantage of being heard by the public; and that when truth and error have fair play, the former is always an overmatch for the latter: hence they cheerfully serve all contending writers that pay them well, without regarding on which side they are of the question in dispute.

6. Being thus continually employed in serving both parties, printers naturally acquire a vast unconcernedness as to the right or wrong opinions contained in what they print; regarding it only as the matter of their daily labor. They print things full of spleen and animosity with the utmost calmness and indifference, and without the least ill-will to the persons reflected on; who

nevertheless unjustly think the printer as much their enemy as the author, and join both together in their resentment.

7. That it is unreasonable to imagine printers approve of everything they print, and to censure them on any particular thing accordingly; since in the way of their business they print such great variety of things opposite and contradictory. It is likewise as unreasonable what some assert, that printers ought not to print anything but what they approve; since if all of that business should make such a resolution, and abide by it, an end would thereby be put to free writing, and the world would afterwards have nothing to read but what happened to be the opinions of printers.

8. That if all printers were determined not to print anything till they were sure it would offend nobody, there would be very little printed.

9. That if they sometimes print vicious or silly things not worth reading, it may not be because they approve such things themselves, but because the people are so viciously and corruptly educated that good things are not encouraged. I have known a very numerous impression of Robin Hood's Songs go off in this province at 2s. per book, in less than a twelvemonth; when a small quantity of David's Psalms (an excellent version) have lain upon my hands above twice the time.

10. That notwithstanding what might be urged in behalf of a man's being allowed to do in the way of his business whatever he is paid for, yet printers do continually discourage the printing of great numbers of bad things, and stifle them in the birth. I myself have constantly refused to print anything that might countenance vice or promote immorality; though by complying in such cases with the corrupt taste of the majority I might have got much money. I have also always refused to

print such things as might do real injury to any person, how much soever I have been solicited and tempted with offers of great pay, and how much soever I have by refusing got the ill-will of those who would have employed me. I have hitherto fallen under the resentment of large bodies of men for refusing absolutely to print any of their party or personal reflections. In this manner I have made myself many enemies, and the constant fatigue of denying is almost insupportable. But the public being unacquainted with all this, whenever the poor printer happens either through ignorance or much persuasion to do anything that is generally thought worthy of blame, he meets with no more friendship or favor on the above account than if there were no merit in it at all. Thus, as Waller says,

> Poets lose half the praise they would have got
> Were it but known what they discreetly blot;

yet are censured for every bad line found in their works with the utmost severity ....

– From the *Pennsylvania Gazette*
June 10 1731

ON SCANDAL

Mr. Gazetteer: I was highly pleased with your last week's paper upon SCANDAL, as the uncommon doctrine therein preached is agreeable both to my principles and practice, and as it was published very seasonably to reprove the impertinence of a writer in the foregoing Thursday's *Mercury* who, at the conclusion of one of his silly paragraphs, laments forsooth that the fair sex are so peculiarly guilty of this enormous crime. Every blockhead, ancient and modern, that could handle a pen has, I think, taken upon him to cant in the same senseless strain. If to *scandalize* be really a crime, what do these puppies mean? They describe it, they dress it up in the most odious, frightful, and detestable colors, they represent it as the worst of crimes, and then roundly and charitably charge the whole race of womankind with it. Are not they then guilty of what they condemn at the same time that they condemn it? If they accuse us of any other crime they must necessarily scandalize while they do it; but to scandalize us with being guilty of scandal is in itself an egregious absurdity, and can proceed from nothing but the most consummate impudence in conjunction with the most profound stupidity.

This supposing, as they do, that to scandalize is a crime, you have convinced all reasonable people is an opinion absolutely erroneous. Let us leave, then, these select mock-moralists, while I entertain you with some account of my life and manners.

I am a young girl of about thirty-five, and live at present with my mother. I have no care upon my head of getting a living, and therefore find it my duty as well as inclination to exercise my talent at censure, for the good of my country-folks. There was, I am told, a certain generous emperor who, if a day had passed over his head in which he had conferred no benefit on any man, used to say to his friends in Latin, *Diem perdidi*, that is, it seems, *I have lost a day*. I believe I should make use of the same expression if it were possible for a day to pass in which I had not, or missed, an opportunity to scandalize somebody; but thanks be praised no such misfortune has befell me these dozen years.

Yet whatever good I may do, I cannot pretend that I at first entered into the practice of this virtue from a principle of public spirit; for I remember that when a child, I had a violent inclination to be ever talking in my own praise; and being continually told that it was ill manners, and once severely whipped for it, the confined stream formed for itself a new channel, and I began to speak for the future in the dispraise of others. This I found more agreeable to company and almost as much so to myself; for what great difference can there be between putting yourself up, or putting your neighbor down? *Scandal,* like other virtues, is in part its own reward, as it gives us the satisfaction of making ourselves appear better than others, or others no better than ourselves.

My mother, good woman, and I have heretofore differed upon this account. She argued that scandal spoilt all good conversation; and I insisted that without it there would be no such thing. Our disputes once rose so high that we parted tea-tables, and I concluded to entertain my acquaintance in the kitchen. The first day of this separation we both drank tea at the same time, but she with her visitors in the parlor.

She would not hear of the last objection to any one's character, but began a new sort of discourse in some such queer philosophical manner as this: "I am mightily pleased sometimes," says she, "when I observe and consider that the world is not so bad as people out of humor imagine it to be. There is something amiable, some good quality or other, in everybody. If we were only to speak of people that are least respected, there is such a one is very dutiful to her father and methinks has a fine set of teeth; such a one is very respectful to her husband; such a one is very kind to her poor neighbors, and besides has a very handsome shape; such a one is always ready to serve a friend and, in my opinion, there is not a woman in town that has a more agreeable air or gait." This fine kind of talk, which lasted near half an hour, she concluded by saying, "I do not doubt but every one of you has made the like observations, and I should be glad to have the conversation continued upon this subject."

Just at this juncture I peeped in at the door, and never in my life before saw such a set of simple, vacant countenances. They looked somehow neither glad nor sorry, nor angry nor pleased, nor indifferent nor attentive; but (excuse the simile) like so many images of rye dough. I, in the kitchen, had already begun a ridiculous story of Mr. – 's intrigue with his maid and his wife's behavior on the discovery; at some of the passages we laughed heartily; and one of the gravest of mamma's company, without making any answer to her discourse, got up *to go and see what the girls were so merry about.* She was followed by a second, and shortly by a third, till at last the old gentlewoman found herself quite alone and, being convinced that her project was impracticable, came herself and finished her tea with us; ever since which *Saul also has been among the prophets,* and our disputes lie dormant. . . .

But, alas! two great evils have lately befallen me at the same time; an extreme cold that I can scarce speak, and a most terrible toothache that I dare hardly open my mouth. For some days past, I have received ten stories for one I have paid; and I am not able to balance my accounts without your assistance. I have long thought that if you would make your paper a vehicle of scandal, you would double the number of your subscribers. I send you herewith accounts of four knavish tricks, two***, five*****, three drubbed wives, and four henpecked husbands, all within this fortnight; which you may, as articles of news, deliver to the public and, if my toothache continues, I shall send you more, being in the mean time your constant reader,

Alice Addertongue.

I thank my correspondent Mrs. Addertongue, for her good will, but desire to be excused inserting the articles of news she has sent me, such things being in reality no news at all.

– From the *Pennsylvania Gazette*
1732

When I disengaged myself, as above mentioned, from private business*, I flattered myself that, by the sufficient though moderate fortune I had acquired, I had secured leisure during the rest of my life for philosophical studies and amusements. I purchased all Dr. Spence's apparatus, who had come from England to lecture here, and I proceeded in my electrical experiments with great alacrity; but the public, now considering me as a man of leisure, laid hold of me for their purposes, every part of our civil government, and almost at the same time, imposing some duty upon me. The governor put me into the commission of the peace; the corporation of the city chose me of the common council, and soon after an alderman; and the citizens at large chose me a burgess to represent them in Assembly. This latter station was the more agreeable to me, as I was at length tired with sitting there to hear debates, in which, as clerk, I could take no part, and which were often so unentertaining that I was induced to amuse myself with making magic squares or circles, or anything to avoid weariness; and I conceived my becoming a member would enlarge my power of doing good. I would not, however, insinuate that my ambition was not flattered by all these promotions; it certainly was; for, considering my low beginning, they were great things to me; and they were still more pleasing, as being so many spontaneous testimonies of the public good opinion, and by me entirely unsolicited. . . .

In 1751, Dr. Thomas Bond**, a particular friend of

---

* In 1748 Franklin acquired a partner, David Hall, who took all the work connected with his printing business off his hands and paid him a share of the profits. The arrangement was a success, and continued for eighteen years.

** Dr. Thomas Bond was the physician with whom Franklin founded the first hospital in Philadelphia.

mine, conceived the idea of establishing a hospital in Philadelphia (a very beneficent design, which has been ascribed to me, but was originally his), for the reception and cure of poor sick persons, whether inhabitants of the province or strangers. He was zealous and active in endeavoring to procure subscriptions for it, but the proposal being a novelty in America, and at first not well understood, he met with but small success.

At length he came to me with the compliment that he found there was no such thing as carrying a public-spirited project through without my being concerned in it.

"For," says he, "I am often asked by those to whom I propose subscribing. Have you consulted Franklin upon this business? And what does he think of it? And when I tell them that I have not (supposing it rather out of your line) they do not subscribe, but say they will consider of it."

I inquired into the nature and probable utility of his scheme, and receiving from him a very satisfactory explanation, I not only subscribed to it myself, but engaged heartily in the design of procuring subscriptions from others. Previously, however to the solicitation, I endeavored to prepare the minds of the people by writing on the subject in the newspapers, which was my usual custom in such cases, but which he had omitted.

The subscriptions afterwards were more free and generous; but beginning to flag, I saw they would be insufficient without some assistance from the Assembly, and therefore proposed to petition for it, which was done. The country members did not at first relish the project; they objected that it could only be serviceable to the city, and therefore the citizens alone should be at the expense of it; and they doubted whether the citizens themselves generally approved of it. My allegation on the contrary, that it met with such approbation as to leave no doubt of our being able to raise two thousand pounds by voluntary donations, they considered as a most extravagant supposition, and utterly impossible.

On this I formed my plan; and, asking leave to bring in a bill for incorporating the contributors according to the prayer of their petition, and granting them a blank sum of money, which leave was obtained chiefly on the consideration that the House could throw the bill out if they did not like it, I drew it so as to make the important clause a conditional one, *viz.*,

And be it enacted, by the authority aforesaid, that when the said contributors shall have met and chosen their managers and treasurer, and shall have raised by their contributions a capital stock of value *(the yearly interest of which is to be applied to the accommodating of the sick poor in the said hospital, free of charge for diet, attendance, advice, and medicines)* and shall make the same appear to the satisfaction of the speaker of the Assembly for the time being, *that* then *it shall and may be lawful for the said speaker, and he is hereby required, to sign an order on the provincial treasurer for the payment of two thousand pounds, in two yearly payments, to the treasurer of the said hospital, to be applied to the founding, building, and finishing of the same.*

This condition carried the bill through; for the members, who had opposed the grant, and now conceived they might have the credit of being charitable without the expense, agreed to its passage; and then, in soliciting subscriptions among the people, we urged the conditional promise of the law as an additional motive to give, since every man's donation would be doubled; thus the clause worked both ways. The subscriptions accordingly soon exceeded the requisite sum, and we claimed and received the public gift, which enabled us to carry the design into execution. A convenient and handsome building was soon erected; the institution has by constant experience been found useful, and flourishes to this day; and I do not remember any of my political maneuvers, the success of which gave me at the time more pleasure, or wherein, after thinking of it, I more easily excused myself for having made some use of cunning.

– From the *Autobiography*
1788

ON SELF-PRAISE

What you mention concerning the love of praise is indeed very true; it reigns more or less in every heart; though we are generally hypocrites in that respect, and pretend to disregard praise, and our nice, modest ears are offended forsooth, with what one of the ancients calls *the sweetest kind of music.* This hypocrisy is only a sacrifice to the pride of others or to their envy; both of which, I think, ought rather to be mortified. The same sacrifice we make when we forbear to *praise ourselves,* which naturally we are all inclined to; and I suppose it was formerly the fashion, or Virgil, that courtly writer, would not have put a speech into the mouth of his hero which nowadays we should esteem so great an indeceny:

> *Sum pius Æneas . . .*
> *. . . fama super æthera notus*.*

One of the Romans, I forget who, justified speaking in his own praise by saying, *Every freeman had a right to speak what he thought of himself as well as of others.* That this is a natural inclination appears in that all children show it and say freely, *I am a good boy; Am I not a good girl?* and the like, till they have been frequently chid and told their trumpeter is dead; and that it is unbecoming to sound their own praise, etc. But *naturam ex-*

---

* I am the dutiful Aeneas . . . whose fame reaches to the clouds.

pellas furca, tamen usque recurret*. Being forbid to praise themselves, they learn instead of it to censure others; which is only a roundabout way of praising themselves; for condemning the conduct of another in any particular amounts to as much as saying, *I am so honest or wise or good or prudent that I could not do or approve of such an action.* This fondness for ourselves rather than malevolence to others, I take to be the general source of censure and backbiting; and I wish man had not been taught to dam up natural currents, to the overflowing and damage of their neighbors' grounds.

Another advantage, methinks, would arise from freely speaking our good thoughts of ourselves, *viz.* if we were wrong in them somebody or other would readily set us right; but now, while we conceal so carefully our vain, erroneous self-opinions, we may carry them to our grave, for who would offer physic to a man that seems to be in good health? And the privilege of recounting freely our own good actions might be an inducement to the doing of them, that we might be enabled to speak of them without being subject to be justly contradicted or charged with falsehood; whereas now, as we are not allowed to mention them, and it is an uncertainty whether others will take due notice of them or not, we are perhaps more indifferent about them; so that, upon the whole, I wish the out-of-fashion practice of praising ourselves would, like other old fashions, come round into fashion again.

But this I fear will not be in our time, so we must even be contented with what little praise we can get from one another. And I will endeavor to make you some amends for the trouble of reading this long scrawl by telling you that I have the sincerest esteem for you as an ingenious man and a good one, which together make the valuable member of society.

– Letter to Jared Eliot
September 12 1751

* Nature excluded still returns again.

POOR RICHARD'S ALMANAC

In 1732 I first published my Almanac, under the name of *Richard Saunders;* it was continued by me about twenty-five years, commonly called *Poor Richard's Almanac.* I endeavored to make it both entertaining and useful, and it accordingly came to be in such demand, that I reaped considerable profit from it, vending annually near ten thousand. And observing that it was generally read, scarce any neighborhood in the province being without it, I considered it as a proper vehicle for conveying instruction among the common people, who bought scarcely any other books; I therefore filled all the little spaces that occurred between the remarkable days in the calendar with proverbial sentences, chiefly such as inculcated industry and frugality, as the means of procuring wealth, and thereby securing virtue; it being more difficult for a man in want, to act always honestly, as, to use here one of those proverbs, *it is hard for an empty sack to stand upright.*

These proverbs, which contained the wisdom of many ages and nations, I assembled and formed into a connected discourse prefixed to the Almanac of 1757*, as the harangue of a wise old man to the people attending an auction. The bringing all these scattered counsels thus into a focus enabled them to make greater impression. The piece, being universally approved, was copied in all the newspapers of the Continent; reprinted in Britain on a broadside, to be stuck up in houses; two translations were made of it in French, and great numbers bought by the clergy and gentry to distribute gratis among their poor parishioners and tenants. In Pennsylvania, as it discouraged useless expense in foreign superfluities, some thought it had its share of influence in producing that growing plenty

---

* An excerpt from this preface is contained in this collection. Franklin's memory failed him, however. He wrote the preface in 1757 for the 1758 Almanac.

of money which was observable for several years after its publication.

I considered my newspaper, also, as another means of communicating instruction, and in that view frequently reprinted in it extracts from the *Spectator* and other moral writers; and sometimes published little pieces of my own, which had been first composed for reading in our *Junto*. Of these are a Socratic dialogue, tending to prove that, whatever might be his parts and abilities, a vicious man could not properly be called a man of sense; and a discourse on self-denial, showing that virtue was not secure till its practice became a habitude and was free from the opposition of contrary inclinations. These may be found in the papers about the beginning of 1735.

In the conduct of my newspaper, I carefully excluded all libeling and personal abuse, which is of late years become so disgraceful to our country. Whenever I was solicited to insert anything of that kind, and the writers pleaded, as they generally did, the liberty of the press, and that a newspaper was like a stagecoach, in which any one who would pay had a right to a place, my answer was, that I would print the piece separately if desired, and the author might have as many copies as he pleased to distribute himself, but that I would not take upon me to spread his detraction; and that, having contracted with my subscribers to furnish them with what might be either useful or entertaining, I could not fill their papers with private altercation, in which they had no concern, without doing them manifest injustice.

Now, many of our printers make no scruple of gratifying the malice of individuals by false accusations of the fairest characters among ourselves, augmenting animosity even to the producing of duels; and are, moreover, so indiscreet as to print scurrilous reflections on the government of neighboring states, and even on the conduct of our best national allies, which may be attended with the most pernicious consequences. These things I mention as a caution to young printers, and that they may be encouraged not to pollute their presses and disgrace their profession by such infamous practices, but refuse steadily, as they may see by my example that such a course of conduct will not, on the whole, be injurious to their interests. . . .

> – From the *Autobiography, Part III*
> 1788

THE WAY TO WEALTH

Courteous Reader: I have heard nothing gives an author so great pleasure as to find his works respectfully quoted by other learned authors. This pleasure I have seldom enjoyed.

For though I have been, if I may say it without vanity, an eminent author of almanacs annually now for a full quarter of a century, my brother authors in the same way, for what reason I know not, have ever been very sparing in their applauses and no other author has taken the least notice of me; so that did not my writings produce me some solid pudding, the great deficiency of praise would have quite discouraged me.

I concluded at length the people were the best judges of my merit, for they buy my works; and besides, in my rambles, where I am not personally known, I have frequently heard one or other of my adages repeated, with *as Poor Richard says* at the end of it. This gave me some satisfaction, as it showed not only that my instructions were regarded, but discovered likewise some respect for my authority; and I own that to encourage the practice of remembering and repeating those sentences, I have sometimes quoted myself with great gravity.

Judge, then, how much I must have been gratified by an accident I am going to relate to you. I stopped my horse lately where a great number of people were collected at a vendue of merchant's goods. The hour of sale not being come, they were conversing on the badness of the times; and one of the company called to a plain, clean old man with white locks,

"Pray, Father Abraham, what think you of the times? Won't these heavy taxes quite ruin the country? How shall we ever be able to pay them? What would you advise us to?"

Father Abraham stood up and replied,

"If you would have my advice, I will give it to you in short; for *a word to the wise is enough,* and *many words won't fill a bushel,* as Poor Richard says."

They all joined, desiring him to speak his mind, and gathering round him he proceeded as follows:

"Friends and neighbors, the taxes are indeed very heavy, and if those laid on by the government were the only ones we had to pay, we might the more easily discharge them; but we have many others, and much more grievous to some of us. We are taxed twice as much by our idleness, three times as much by our pride, and four times as much by our folly; and from these taxes the commissioners cannot ease or deliver us by allowing an abatement. However, let us hearken to good advice, and something may be done for us. *God helps them that help themselves,* as Poor Richard says in his almanac of 1733.

"It would be thought a hard government that should tax its people one-tenth part of their time, to be employed in its service, but idleness taxes many of us much more, if we reckon all that is spent in absolute sloth or doing of nothing, with that which is spent in idle employments or amusements that amount to nothing. Sloth, by bringing on diseases, absolutely shortens life. *Sloth, like rust, consumes faster than labor wears; while the used key is always bright,* as Poor Richard says. *But dost thou love life? then do not squander time, for that's the stuff life is made of,* as Poor Richard says.

"How much more than is necessary do we spend in

sleep? forgetting that *the sleeping fox catches no poultry* and that *there will be sleeping enough in the grave,* as Poor Richard says. . . .

"Methinks I hear some of you say: 'Must a man afford himself no leisure?' I will tell thee, my friend, what Poor Richard says: *employ thy time well if thou meanest to gain leisure;* and *since thou art not sure of a minute, throw not away an hour!* Leisure is time for doing something useful; this leisure the diligent man will obtain, but the lazy man never; so that, as Poor Richard says, *a life of leisure and a life of laziness are two things.* Do you imagine that sloth will afford you more comfort than labor? No! for, as Poor Richard says, *trouble springs from idleness and grievous toil from needless ease.* . . .

"Trusting too much to others' care is the ruin of many; for, as the almanac says, *in the affairs of this world men are saved, not by faith, but by the want of it;* but a man's own care is profitable; for, saith Poor Dick, *learning is to the studious and riches to the careful;* as well as *power to the bold* and *heaven to the virtuous.* And further, *if you would have a faithful servant and one that you like, serve yourself.*

"And again, he adviseth to circumspection and care, even in the smallest matters; because sometimes *a little neglect may breed great mischief;* adding, *for want of a nail the shoe was lost; for want of a shoe the horse was lost; and for want of a horse the rider was lost;* being over-taken and slain by the enemy; all for want of a little care about a horseshoe nail! . . .

"*If you would be wealthy,* says he in another almanac, *think of saving as well as of getting. The Indies have not made Spain rich, because her outgoes are greater than her incomes.*

"Away, then, with your expensive follies, and you will not have so much cause to complain of hard times, heavy taxes, and chargeable families, for, as Poor Dick says,

> *Women and wine, game and deceit,*
> *Make the wealth small and the wants great.*

"And further, *what maintains one vice would bring up two children.* You may think, perhaps, that a little tea or a little punch now and then, a diet a little more costly, clothes a little finer, and a little more entertainment now and then, can be no great matter; but remember what Poor Richard says: *many a little makes a mickle;* and further, *beware of little expenses; a small leak will sink a great ship,* and again, *who dainties love shall beggars prove;* and moreover, *fools make feasts and wise men eat them.*

"Here are you all got together at this vendue of fineries and knick-knacks. You call them goods; but if you do not take care they will prove evils to some of you. . . .

"And after all, of what use is this pride of appearance, for which so much is risked, so much is suffered? It cannot promote health or ease pain; it makes no increase of merit in the person; it creates envy; it hastens misfortune.

> *What is a butterfly? At best*
> *He's but a caterpillar drest,*
> *The gaudy fop's his picture just,*

as Poor Richard says.

"But what madness must it be to run into debt for these superfluities! We are offered by the terms of this vendue six months' credit; and that, perhaps, has induced some of us to attend it, because we cannot spare the ready money and hope now to be fine without it. But ah! think what you do when you run in debt: you give to another power over your liberty. If you cannot pay at the time, you will be ashamed to see your creditor; you will be in fear when you speak to him; you will make poor, pitiful, sneaking excuses, and by degrees come to lose your veracity and sink into base, downright lying; for, as Poor Richard says, *the second vice is lying, the first is running into debt;* and again, to the same purpose, *lying rides upon debt's back;* whereas a free-born Englishman ought not to be ashamed or afraid to see or speak to any man living. But poverty often deprives a man of all spirit and virtue. *'Tis hard for an empty bag to stand upright,* as Poor Richard truly says. . . .

"And now to conclude, *experience keeps a dear school, but fools will learn in no other, and scarce in that;* for it is true, *we may give advice, but we cannot give conduct,* as Poor Richard says. However, remember this: *they that won't be counseled can't be helped,* as Poor Richard says; and further, that *if you will not hear reason she'll surely rap your knuckles.*"

Thus the old gentleman ended his harangue. The people heard it and approved the doctrine, and immediately practiced the contrary, just as if it had been a common sermon. For the vendue opened and they began to buy extravagantly, notwithstanding all his cautions and their own fear of taxes. I found the good man had thoroughly studied my almanacs and digested all I had dropped on those topics during the course of twenty-five years. The frequent mention he made of me must have tired any one else; but my vanity was wonderfully delighted with it, though I was conscious that not a tenth part of the wisdom was my own which he ascribed to me, but rather the gleanings that I had made of the sense of all ages and nations.

However, I resolved to be the better for the echo of it, and though I had at first determined to buy stuff for a new coat, I went away resolved to wear my old one a little longer.

Reader, if thou wilt do the same, thy profit will be as great as mine. I am, as ever, thine to serve thee,

Richard Saunders

– Preface to *Poor Richard's Almanac* for 1758

53

How to make a Striking Sundial, by which not only a man's Family, but all his Neighbors for ten Miles round may know what o' Clock it is, when the Sun shines, without seeing the Dial.

Choose an open Place in your Yard or Garden, on which the Sun may shine all Day without any Impediment from Trees or Buildings. On the Ground mark out your Hour Lines, as for a horizontal Dial, according to Art, taking Room enough for the Guns. On the Line for One o'Clock place one Gun; on the Two o'Clock Line two Guns, and so of the rest. The Guns must all be charged with Powder, but Ball is unnecessary. Your Gnomon or Style must have twelve burning Glasses annex'd to it, and be so placed that the Sun shining through the Glasses, one after the other, shall cause the Focus or burning Spot to fall on the Hour Line of One, for Example, at One o' Clock, and there kindle a Train of Gunpowder that shall fire one Gun. At Two o' Clock, a Focus shall fall on the Hour Line of Two, and kindle another Train that shall discharge two Guns successively; and so of the rest.

Note: There must be 78 Guns in all. Thirty-two Pounders will be best for this Use; but 18 Pounders may do, and will cost less, as well as use less Powder, for nine Pounds of Powder will do for one Charge of each eighteen Pounder; whereas the Thirty-two Pounder would require for each Gun 16 Pounds.

Note also: That the chief Expense will be the Powder, for the Cannon once bought will, with Care, last 100 Years.

Note moreover: That there will be a great Saving of Powder in Cloudy Days.

Kind Reader, Methinks I hear thee say, That is Indeed a good Thing to know how the Time passes, but this Kind of Dial, notwithstanding the mentioned Savings, would be very Expensive, and the Cost greater than the Advantage.

Thou art wise, my Friend, to be so considerate before-hand; some Fools would not have found out so much till they had made the Dial and tried it. . . . Let all such learn that many a private and many a public Project are like this Striking Dial, great Cost for little Profit.

– From *Poor Richard's Almanac*
1757

ON CIVIC IMPROVEMENTS

Our city, though laid out with beautiful regularity, the streets large, straight, and crossing each other at right angles, had the disgrace of suffering those streets to remain long unpaved, and in wet weather the wheels of heavy carriages ploughed them into a quagmire, so that it was difficult to cross them; and in dry weather the dust was offensive. I had lived near what was called the Jersey Market, and saw with pain the inhabitants wading in mud while purchasing their provisions. A strip of ground down the middle of that market was at length paved with brick so that, being once in the market, they had firm footing, but were often over shoes in dirt to get there.

By talking and writing on the subject, I was at length instrumental in getting the street paved with stone between the market and the bricked foot-pavement, that was on each side next the houses. This for some time gave an easy access to the market dry-shod; but, the rest of the street not being paved, whenever a carriage came out of the mud upon this pavement it shook off and left its dirt upon it, and it was soon covered with mire, which was not removed, the city as yet having no scavengers.

After some inquiry, I found a poor, industrious man, who was willing to undertake keeping the pavement clean by sweeping it twice a week, carrying off the dirt from before all the neighbors' doors, for the sum of sixpence per month, to be paid by each house. I then wrote and printed a paper setting forth the advantages to the neighborhood that might be obtained by this small expense; the greater ease in keeping our houses clean, so much dirt not being brought in by people's feet; the benefit to the shops by more custom, etc., as buyers could more easily get at them; and by not having, in windy weather, the dust blown in upon their goods, etc.

I sent one of these papers to each house, and in a day or two went round to see who would subscribe an agreement to pay these sixpences; it was unanimously signed, and for a time well executed. All the inhabitants of the city were delighted with the cleanliness of the pavement that surrounded the market, it being a convenience to all, and this raised a general desire to have all the streets paved, and made the people more willing to submit to a tax for that purpose.

After some time I drew a bill for paving the city, and brought it into the Assembly. It was just before I went to England, in 1757, and did not pass till I was gone, and then with an alteration in the mode of assessment which I thought not for the better, but with an additional provision for lighting as well as paving the streets, which was a great improvement. It was by a private person, the late Mr. John Clifton, his giving a sample of the utility of lamps by placing one at his door, that the people were first impressed with the idea of enlighting all the city. The honor of this public benefit has also been ascribed to me, but it belongs truly to that gentleman.

I did but follow his example, and have only some merit to claim respecting the form of our lamps, as differing from the globe lamps we were at first supplied with from London. Those we found inconvenient in these respects; they admitted no air below; the smoke, therefore, did not readily go out above, but circulated in the globe, lodged on its inside, and soon obstructed the light they were intended to afford; giving, besides, the daily trouble of wiping them clean; and an accidental stroke on one of them would demolish it, and render it totally useless.

I therefore suggested the composing them of four flat panes with a long funnel above to draw up the smoke, and crevices admitting air below to facilitate the ascent of the smoke; by this means they were kept clean, and did not grow dark in a few hours as the London lamps do, but continued bright till morning, and an accidental stroke would generally break but a single pane, easily repaired. . . .

The mention of these improvements puts me in mind of one I proposed, when in London, to Dr. Fothergill, who was among the best men I have known, and a great promoter of useful projects. I had observed that the streets, when dry, were never swept, and the light dust carried away; but it was suffered to accumulate till wet weather reduced it to mud, and then, after lying some days so deep on the pavement that there was no crossing but in paths kept clean by poor people with brooms, it was with great labor raked together and thrown up into carts open above, the sides of which suffered some of the slush at every jolt on the pavement to shake out and fall, sometimes to the annoyance of foot-passengers. The reason given for not sweeping the dusty streets was that the dust would fly into the windows of shops and houses.

An accidental occurrence had instructed me how much sweeping might be done in a little time. I found at my door in Craven Street one morning a poor woman sweeping my pavement with a birch broom; she appeared very pale and feeble, as just come out of a fit of sickness. I asked who employed her to sweep there; she said, "Nobody, but I am very poor and in distress, and I sweeps before gentlefolkses doors, and hopes they will give me something."

I bid her sweep the whole street clean, and I would give her a shilling; this was at nine o'clock; at twelve she came for the shilling. From the slowness I saw at first in her working, I could scarce believe that the work was done so soon, and sent my servant to examine it, who reported that the whole street was swept perfectly clean, and all the dust placed in the gutter, which was in the middle; and the next rain washed it quite away, so that the pavement and even the kennel were perfectly clean.

I then judged that if that feeble woman could sweep such a street in three hours, a strong, active man might have done it in half the time.

Some may think these trifling matters not worth minding or relating; but when they consider that though dust blown into the eyes of a single person, or into a single shop on a windy day, is but of small importance, yet the great number of the instances in a populous city, and its frequent repetitions give it weight and consequence, perhaps they will not censure very severely those who bestow some attention to affairs of this seemingly low nature. Human felicity is produced not so much by great pieces of good fortune that seldom happen, as by little advantages that occur every day. . . .

– From the *Autobiography, Part III*
1788

A NARRATIVE OF THE LATE MASSACRES IN LANCASTER COUNTY

These Indians were the remains of a tribe of the Six Nations, settled at Conestogo, and thence called Conestogo Indians.

On the first arrival of the English in Pennsylvania, messengers from this tribe came to welcome them with presents of venison, corn, and skins; and the whole tribe entered into a treaty of friendship with the first proprietor, William Penn, which was to last "as long as the sun should shine, or the waters run in the rivers."

This treaty has been since frequently renewed and the chain brightened, as they express it, from time to time. It has never been violated, on their part or ours, till now. As their lands by degrees were mostly purchased, and the settlements of the white people began to surround them, the proprietor assigned them lands on the manor of Conestogo, which they might not part with; there they have lived many years in friendship with their white neighbors, who loved them for their peaceable inoffensive behavior.

It has always been observed that Indians settled in the neighborhood of white people do not increase, but diminish continually. This tribe accordingly went on diminishing till there remained in their town on the manor but twenty persons, *viz.* seven men, five women, and eight children, boys and girls.

Of these, Shehaes was a very old man, having assisted at the second treaty held with them by Mr. Penn in 1701, and ever since continued a faithful and affectionate friend to the English. He is said to have been an exceeding good man, considering his education, being naturally of a most kind, benevolent temper.

Peggy was Shehaes's daughter; she worked for her aged father, continuing to live with him, though married, and attended him with filial duty and tenderness.

John was another good old man; his son Harry helped to support him.

George and Will Soc were two brothers, both young men.

John Smith, a valuable young man of the Cayuga nation, who became acquainted with Peggy, Shehaes's daughter some few years since, married, and settled in that family. They had one child, about three years old.

Betty, a harmless old woman; and her son Peter, a likely young lad.

Sally, whose Indian name was Wyanjoy, a woman much esteemed by all that knew her for her prudent and good behavior in some very trying situations of life. She was a truly good and an amiable woman, had no children of her own; but a distant relation dying, she had taken a child of that relation's to bring up as her own, and performed towards it all the duties of an affectionate parent.

The reader will observe that many of their names are English. It is common with the Indians, that have an affection for the English, to give themselves and their children the names of such English persons as they particularly esteem.

This little society continued the custom they had begun, when more numerous, of addressing every new governor, and every descendant of the first proprietor, welcoming him to the province, assuring him of their fidelity, and praying a continuance of that favor and protection they had hitherto experienced. They had accordingly sent up an address of this kind to our present governor, on his arrival; but the same was scarce delivered when the unfortunate catastrophe happened which we are about to relate.

On Wednesday, the 14th of December, 1763, fifty-seven men, from some of our frontier townships who had projected the destruction of this little commonwealth, came, all well mounted and armed with firelocks, hangers, and hatchets, having traveled through the country in the night, to Conestogo manor. There they surrounded the small village of Indian huts, and just at break of day broke into them all at once. Only three men, two women, and a young boy, were found at home, the rest being out among the neighboring white people, some to sell the baskets, brooms, and bowls they manufactured, and others on other occasions. These poor defenceless creatures were immediately fired upon, stabbed and hatcheted to death! The good Shehaes, among the rest, cut to pieces in his bed. All of them were scalped and otherwise horribly mangled. Then their huts were set on fire, and most of them burnt down. Then the troop, pleased with their own conduct and bravery, but enraged that any of the poor Indians had escaped the massacre, rode off, and in small parties, by different roads, went home.

The universal concern of the neighboring white people on hearing of this event, and the lamentations of the younger Indians when they returned and saw the desolation, and the butchered, half-burnt bodies of their murdered parents and other relations, cannot well be expressed.

The magistrates of Lancaster sent out to collect the remaining Indians, brought them into the town for their better security against any farther attempt; and, it is said, condoled with them on the misfortune that had happened, took them by the hand, comforted, and promised them protection. They were all put into the workhouse, a strong building, as the place of greatest safety.

When the shocking news arrived in town, a proclamation was issued by the governor. . . .

Notwithstanding this proclamation, those cruel men again assembled themselves and, hearing that the remaining fourteen Indians were in the workhouse at Lancaster, they suddenly appeared in that town on the 27th of December. Fifty of them, armed as before, dismounting, went directly to the workhouse and by violence broke open the door, and entered with the utmost fury in their countenances. When the poor wretches saw they had no protection nigh, nor could possibly escape, and being without the least weapon for defence, they divided into their little families, the children clinging to the parents; they fell on their knees, protested their innocence, declared their love to the English and that, in their whole lives they had never done them injury; and in this posture they all received the hatchet! Men, women, and little children were every one inhumanly murdered in cold blood!

The barbarous men who committed the atrocious act, in defiance of government, of all laws human and divine, and to the eternal disgrace of their country and color, then mounted their horses, huzzaed in triumph, as if they had gained a victory, and rode off *unmolested!*

The bodies of the murdered were then brought out and exposed in the street till a hole could be made in the earth to receive and cover them.

But the wickedness cannot be covered; the guilt will lie in the whole land, till justice is done on the murderers. The blood of the innocent will cry to Heaven for vengeance.

It is said that Shehaes being before told that it was to be feared some English might come from the frontier into the country, and murder him and his people, he replied, "It is impossible; there are Indians, indeed, in the woods, who would kill me and mine if they could get at us, for my friendship to the English; but the English will wrap me in their matchcoat, and secure me from all danger."

How unfortunately was he mistaken!

Another proclamation has been issued, offering a great reward for apprehending the murderers. . . .

These proclamations have as yet produced no discovery; the murderers having given out such threatenings against those that disapprove their proceedings that the whole country seems to be in terror, and no one dares speak what he knows; even the letters from thence are unsigned, in which any dislike is expressed of the rioters.

There are some (I am ashamed to hear it) who would extenuate the enormous wickedness of these actions by saying, "The inhabitants of the frontiers are exasperated with the murder of their relations by the enemy Indians in the present war."

It is possible; but though this might justify their going out into the woods to seek for those enemies, and avenge upon them those murders, it can never justify their turning into the heart of the country to murder their friends.

If an Indian injures me, does it follow that I may revenge that injury on all Indians? It is well known that Indians are of different tribes, nations, and languages, as well as the white people. In Europe, if the French, who are white people, should injure the Dutch, are they to revenge it on the English because they too are white people? The only crime of these poor wretches seems to have been that they had a reddish-brown skin and black hair; and some people of that sort, it seems, had murdered some of our relations. If it be right to kill men for such a reason, then should any man with a freckled face and red hair kill a wife or child of mine, it would be right for me to revenge it by killing all the freckled, red-haired men, women, and children I could afterwards anywhere meet with. . . .

Do we come to America to learn and practice the manners of barbarians? But this, barbarians as they are, they practice against their enemies only, not against their friends. These poor people have been always our friends. Their fathers received ours, when strangers here, with kindness and hospitality. Behold the return we have made them! When we grew more numerous and powerful, they put themselves under our protection. See, in the mangled corpses of the last remains of the tribe, how effectually we have afforded it to them.

Unhappy people! to have lived in such times, and by such neighbors. . . .

– Philadelphia
1764

SCIENTIST AND INVENTOR

In 1746, being at Boston, I met there with a Dr. Spence who was lately arrived from Scotland, and showed me some electric experiments. They were imperfectly performed, as he was not very expert; but, being on a subject quite new to me, they equally surprised and pleased me. Soon after my return to Philadelphia, our library company received from Mr. P. Collinson, Fellow of the Royal Society of London, a present of a glass tube, with some account of the use of it in making such experiments. I eagerly seized the opportunity of repeating what I had seen at Boston; and, by much practice, acquired great readiness in performing those, also, which we had an account of from England, adding a number of new ones. I say much practice, for my house was continually full with people who came to see these new wonders.

To divide a little this incumbrance among my friends, I caused a number of similar tubes to be blown at our glasshouse, with which they furnished themselves, so that we had at length several performers. Among these, the principal was Mr. Kinnersley, an ingenious neighbor, whom being out of business, I encouraged to undertake showing the experiments for money, and drew up for him two lectures in which the experiments were ranged in such order, and accompanied with such explanations in such method, as that the foregoing should assist in comprehending the following. He procured an elegant apparatus for the purpose, in which all the little machines that I had roughly made for myself were nicely formed by instrument-makers. His lectures were well attended, and gave great satisfaction; and after some time he went through the colonies, exhibiting them in every capital town, and picked up some money. In the West India islands, indeed, it was with difficulty the experiments could be made, from the general moisture of the air.

Obliged as we were to Mr. Collinson for his present

of the tube, etc., I thought it right he should be informed of our success in using it, and wrote him several letters containing accounts of our experiments. He got them read in the Royal Society, where they were not at first thought worth so much notice as to be printed in their Transactions. One paper that I wrote for Mr. Kinnersley on the sameness of lightning with electricity, I sent to Dr. Mitchel, an acquaintance of mine, and one of the members also of that society, who wrote me word that it had been read, but was laughed at by the connoisseurs.

The papers, however, being shown to Dr. Fothergill, he thought them of too much value to be stifled, and advised the printing of them. Mr. Collinson then gave them to Cave for publication in his *Gentleman's Magazine*; but he chose to print them separately in a pamphlet, and Dr. Fothergill wrote the preface. Cave, it seems, judged rightly for his profit, for by the additions that arrived afterwards they swelled to a quarto volume, which has had five editions, and cost him nothing for copy-money.

It was, however, some time before those papers were much taken notice of in England. A copy of them happening to fall into the hands of the Count de Buffon, a philosopher deservedly of great reputation in France and, indeed, all over Europe, he prevailed with M. Dalibard to translate them into French, and they were printed at Paris. The publication offended the Abbé Nollet, preceptor in Natural Philosophy to the royal family, and an able experimenter, who had formed and published a theory of electricity, which then had the general vogue. He could not at first believe that such a work came from America, and said it must have been fabricated by his enemies at Paris, to decry his system. Afterwards, having been assured that there really existed such a person as Franklin in Philadelphia, which he had doubted, he wrote and published a volume of Letters, chiefly addressed to me, defending his theory, and denying the verity of my experiments, and of the positions deduced from them.

I once purposed answering the Abbé, and actually began the answer; but, on consideration that my writings contained a description of experiments which any one might repeat and verify, and if not to be verified, could not be defended; or of observations offered as conjectures, and not delivered dogmatically, therefore not laying me under any obligation to defend them; and reflecting that a dispute between two persons, writing in different languages, might be lengthened greatly by mistranslations, and thence misconceptions of one another's meaning, much of one of the Abbé's letters being founded on an error in the translation, I concluded to let my papers shift for themselves, believing it was better to spend what time I could spare from public business in making new experiments than in disputing about those already made.

I therefore never answered M. Nollet, and the event gave me no cause to repent my silence; for my friend M. le Roy, of the Royal Academy of Sciences, took up my cause and refuted him; my book was translated into the Italian, German, and Latin languages; and the doctrine it contained was by degrees universally adopted by the philosophers of Europe, in preference to that of the Abbé; so that he lived to see himself the last of his sect, except Monsieur B--, of Paris, who was his *élève* and immediate disciple.

What gave my book the more sudden and general celebrity, was the success of one of its proposed experiments, made by Messrs. Dalibard and de Lor at Marly, for drawing lightning from the clouds. This engaged the public attention everywhere. M. de Lor, who had an apparatus for experimental philosophy and lectured in that branch of science, undertook to repeat what he called the *Philadelphia Experiments;* and, after they were performed before the king and court, all the curious of Paris flocked to see them. I will not swell this narrative with an account of that capital experiment, nor of the infinite pleasure I received in the success of a similar one I made soon after with a kite at Philadelphia, as both are to be found in the histories of electricity.

Dr. Wright, an English physician, when at Paris, wrote to a friend, who was of the Royal Society, an account of the high esteem my experiments were in among the learned abroad, and of their wonder that my writings had been so little noticed in England. The Society, on this, resumed the consideration of the letters that had been read to them; and the celebrated Dr. Watson drew up a summary account of them, and of all I had afterwards sent to England on the subject, which he accompanied with some praise of the writer.

This summary was then printed in their Transactions; and some members of the Society in London, particularly the very ingenious Mr. Canton, having verified the experiment of procuring lightning from the clouds by a pointed rod, and acquainting them with the success, they soon made me more than amends for the slight with which they had before treated me. Without my having made any application for that honor, they chose me a member, and voted that I should be excused the customary payments, which would have amounted to twenty-five guineas; and ever since have given me their transactions gratis. They also presented me with the gold medal of Sir Godfrey Copley for the year 1753, the delivery of which was accompanied by a very handsome speech of the president, Lord Macclesfield, wherein I was highly honored. . . .

– From the *Autobiography, Part III*
1788

THE ELECTRICAL KITE

Franklin occupied much of his time in the years between 1746 and 1752 with experiments in electricity, as he relates in his autobiography. His chief contributions were his proof of the identity of lightning and electricity, his theory of positive and negative states of electricity, and his suggestion that houses and ships could be secured against damage by lightning by the erection of pointed rods which would draw off the electricity contained in it. This last was a typical example of his eagerness to make science immediately useful, and made his name a household word in Europe as well as America. To the public a man who could tame the terrifying power of nature seemed a magician; his bold experimentation excited admiration among European scientists, absorbed in theory and logic.

He never wrote the full story of his famous kite experiment. The official account sent to the Royal Society in London is impersonally scientific. The following one was written by him at Philadelphia, October 19 1752.

As frequent mention is made in public papers from Europe of the success of the Philadelphia experiment for drawing the electric fire from clouds by means of pointed rods of iron erected on high buildings, etc., it may be agreeable to the curious to be informed that the same experiment has succeeded in Philadelphia, though made in a different and more easy manner, which is as follows.

Make a small cross of two light strips of cedar, the arms so long as to reach to the four corners of a large thin silk handkerchief when extended; tie the corners of the handkerchief to the extremities of the cross so you have the body of the kite; which, being properly accommodated with a tail, loop and string, will rise in the air like those made of paper; but this being of silk is fitter to bear the wet and wind of a thunder-gust without tearing. To the top of the upright stick of the cross is to be fixed a very sharp-pointed wire, rising a foot or more above the wood. To the end of the twine next the hand is to be tied a silk ribbon, and where the silk and twine join, a key may be fastened. This kite may be raised when a thunder-gust appears to be coming on, and the person who holds the string must stand within a door or window, or under some cover, so that the silk ribbon may not be wet; and care must be taken that the twine does not touch the frame of the door or window. As soon as any of the thunder-clouds come over the kite, the pointed wire will draw the electric fire from them, and the kite, with all the twine, will be electrified, and the loose filaments of the twine will stand out every way, and be attracted by an approaching finger. And when the rain has wetted the kite and twine so that it can conduct the electric fire freely, you will find it stream out plentifully from the key on the approach of your knuckle. At this key the phial may be charged; and from electric fire thus obtained spirits may be kindled, and all the other electric experiments be performed which are usually done by the help of a rubbed glass globe or tube, and thereby the sameness of electric matter with that of lightning completely demonstrated.

– Read at the Royal Society
December 21 1752

BLUNT VS. POINTED
LIGHTNING CONDUCTORS

A controversy arose in England as to the relative merits of blunt and pointed lightning conductors. The King sided with the knobbed school against the political rebel, Franklin. The pointed conductors on the Queen's palace were replaced by blunt ones. Sir John Pringle resigned as President of the Royal Society because he supported Franklin. Asked to comment, Franklin wrote to a friend:

I have never entered into any controversy in defence of my philosophical opinions; I leave them to take their chance in the world. If they are *right*, truth and experience will support them; if wrong, they ought to be refuted and rejected. Disputes are apt to sour one's temper and disturb one's quiet. I have no private interest in the reception of my inventions by the world, having never made nor proposed to make the least profit by any of them. The King's changing his *pointed* conductors for blunt ones is, therefore, a matter of small importance to me. If I had a wish about it, it would be that he had rejected them altogether as ineffectual. For it is only since he thought himself and family safe from the thunder of Heaven that he dared to use his own thunder in destroying his innocent subjects.

– Passy*, October 14 1777

ACCOUNT OF AN ACCIDENT

The full danger of electrical experiments was not realized in Franklin's time. He knew, for example, that wet objects were better conductors than dry ones, but he did not know that if the cord of his kite had been thoroughly wet he might have been electrocuted. A Swedish scientist, Prof. Richmann, working in the Imperial Academy of Sciences in St. Petersburg, actually was electrocuted whil trying to repeat Franklin's Philadelphia experiment t the following, Franklin describes a dramatic narrow es pe.

I have lately made an experiment in electricit that I desire never to repeat. Two nights ago, being about to kill a turkey by the shock from two large glas jars, containing as much electrical fire as forty comn n phials, I inadvertently took the whole through my vn arms and

* At that time, Passy was a village abou three miles from Paris, where Franklin had his villa. It is now rt of Paris.

72

body, by receiving the fire from the united top wires with one hand while the other held a chain connected with the outsides of both jars. The company present (whose talking to me and to one another, I suppose occasioned my in-attention to what I was about) say that the flash was very great, and the crack as loud as a pistol; yet, my senses being instantly gone, I neither saw the one nor heard the other; nor did I feel the stroke on my hand, though afterwards I found it raised a round swelling where the fire entered, as big as half a pistol bullet; by which you may judge of the quickness of the electrical fire, which by this instance seems to be greater than that of sound, light, or animal sensation.

What I can remember of the matter is that I was about to try whether the bottles or jars were fully charged by the strength and length of the stream issuing to my hand, as I commonly used to do and which I might safely enough have done if I had not held the chain in the other hand. I then felt what I know not how well to describe; a universal blow throughout my whole body from head to foot, which seemed within as well as without; after which the first thing I took notice of was a violent quick shaking of my body, which gradually remitting, my sense as gradually returned, and then I thought the bottles must be discharged, but could not conceive how, till at last I perceived the chain in my hand and recollected what I had been about to do. That part of my hand and fingers which held the chain was left white, as though the blood had been driven out, and remained so eight or ten minutes after, feeling like dead flesh; and I had a numbness in my arms and the back of my neck which continued till the next morning but wore off. Nothing remains now of this shock but a soreness in my breast-bone, which feels as if I had been bruised. I did not fall, but suppose I should have been knocked down if I had received the stroke in my head.

The whole was over in less than a minute.

You may communicate this to Mr. Bowdoin*, as a caution to him, but do not make it more public, for I am ashamed to have been guilty of so notorious a blunder; a match for that of the Irishman whom my sister told me of who, to divert his wife, poured the bottle of gunpowder on the live coal; or of that other who, being about to steal powder, made a hole in the cask with a hot iron.

> – To an unidentified friend in Boston
> Philadelphia, December 25 1750

FOLLOWING A WHIRLWIND

Being in Maryland, riding with Colonel Tasker and some other gentlemen to his country-seat, where I and my son were entertained by that amiable and worthy man with great hospitality and kindness, we saw, in the vale below us, a small whirlwind beginning in the road and showing itself by the dust it raised and contained. It appeared in the form of a sugar-loaf, spinning on its point, moving up the hill towards us, and enlarging as it came forward. When it passed by us, its smaller part near the ground appeared no bigger than a common barrel; but widening upwards, it seemed, at forty or fifty feet high, to be twenty or thirty feet in diameter. The rest of the company stood looking after it; but my curiosity being stronger, I followed it, riding close by its side, and observed its licking up in its progress all the dust that was under its smaller part. As it is a common opinion that a shot, fired through a water-spout, will break it, I tried to break this little whirlwind by striking my whip frequently through it, but without any effect. Soon after, it quitted the road and took into the woods, growing every moment larger and stronger,

* James Bowdoin, at this time twenty-three years old, later became the first president of the American Academy of Arts and Sciences and governor of Massachusetts.

raising instead of dust the old dry leaves with which the ground was thick covered, and making a great noise with them and the branches of the trees, bending some tall trees round in a circle swiftly and very surprisingly, though the progressive motion of the whirl was not so swift but that a man on foot might have kept pace with it; but the circular motion was amazingly rapid. By the leaves it was now filled with, I could plainly perceive that the current of air they were driven by moved upwards in a spiral line; and when I saw the trunks and bodies of large trees enveloped in the passing whirl, which continued entire after it had left them, I no longer wondered that my whip had no effect on it in its smaller state. I accompanied it about three-quarters of a mile, till some limbs of dead trees, broken off by the whirl, flying about and falling near me made me more apprehensive of danger; and then I stopped, looking at the top of it as it went on, which was visible, by means of the leaves contained in it, for a very great height above the trees. Many of the leaves, as they got loose from the upper and widest part, were scattered in the wind; but so great was their height in the air that they appeared no bigger than flies.

My son, who was by this time come up with me, followed the whirlwind till it left the woods, and crossed an old tobacco-field, where, finding neither dust nor leaves to take up, it gradually became invisible below, as it went away over the field. The course of the general wind then blowing was along with us as we traveled, and the progressive motion of the whirlwind was in a direction nearly opposite, though it did not keep a straight line, nor was its progressive motion uniform, it making little sallies on either hand as it went, proceeding sometimes faster and sometimes slower, and seeming sometimes for a few seconds almost stationary, then starting forward pretty fast again. When we rejoined the company, they were admiring the vast height of the leaves now brought by the common wind over our heads. These leaves accompanied us as we traveled, some falling now and then round about us, and some not reaching the ground till we had gone near three miles from the place where we first saw the whirlwind begin. Upon asking Colonel Tasker if such whirlwinds were common in Maryland, he answered: "No, not at all common; but we got this on purpose to treat Mr. Franklin."

–Philadelphia, August 25 1755

OBSERVATIONS ON INSECTS

Your observation on what you* have lately read concerning insects is very just and solid. Superficial minds are apt to despise those who make that part of the creation their study, as mere triflers; but certainly the world has been much obliged to them. Under the care and management of man, the labors of the little silkworm afford employment and subsistence to thousands of families, and become an immense article of commerce. The bee, too, yields us its delicious honey, and its wax useful to a multitude of purposes. Another insect, it is said, produces the cochineal, from whence we have our rich scarlet dye. The usefulness of the cantharides, or Spanish flies, in medicine is known to all, and thousands owe their lives to that knowledge. By human industry and observation, other properties of other insects may possibly be hereafter discovered, and of equal utility. A thorough acquaintance with the nature of these little creatures may also enable mankind to prevent the increase of such as are noxious, or secure us against the mischiefs they occasion. These

* Mary Stevenson, later Mary Stevenson Hewson, was the daughter of Franklin's Craven Street landlady, in whose house he lived during his seventeen years in London. He was disappointed in his hopes of a match between Mary and his son William, but he continued to regard her as a daughter. After she left home they corresponded on philosophical subjects, at her request.

things doubtless your books make mention of; I can only add a particular late instance which I had from a Swedish gentleman of good credit. In the green timber, intended for ship-building at the King's yards in that country, a kind of worm was found which every year became more numerous and more pernicious, so that the ships were greatly damaged before they came into use. The King sent Linnaeus, the great naturalist, from Stockholm, to inquire into the affair, and see if the mischief was capable of any remedy. He found, on examination, that the worm was produced from a small egg, deposited in the little roughnesses on the surface of the wood by a particular kind of fly or beetle; from whence the worm, as soon as it was hatched, began to eat into the substance of the wood, and after some time came out again a fly of the parent kind, and so the species increased. The season in which the fly laid its eggs, Linnaeus knew to be about a fortnight (I think) in the month of May, and at no other time in the year. He therefore advised that some days before that season all the green timber should be thrown into the water, and kept under water till the season was over. Which being done by the King's order, the flies missing their usual nests could not increase; and the species was either destroyed or went elsewhere; and the wood was effectually preserved, for after the first year, it became too dry and hard for their purpose.

There is, however, a prudent moderation to be used in studies of this kind. The knowledge of nature may be ornamental, and it may be useful; but if, to attain an eminence in that, we neglect the knowledge and practice of essential duties, we deserve reprehension. For there is no rank in natural knowledge of equal dignity and importance with that of being a good parent, a good child, a good husband or wife, a good neighbor or friend, a good subject or citizen. . . .

– From a letter to Mary Stevenson
London, June 11 1760

Dear Brother: I like your ballad and I think it well adapted for your purpose of discountenancing expensive foppery, and encouraging industry and frugality. If you can get it generally sung in your country, it may probably have a good deal of the effect you hope and expect from it. But, as you aimed at making it general, I wonder you chose so uncommon a measure in poetry that none of the tunes in common use will suit it. Had you fitted it to an old one, well known, it must have spread much faster than I doubt it will do from the best new tune we can get composed for it . . . I will however get it as well done for you as I can.

Do not imagine that I mean to deprecate the skill of our composers of music here; they are admirable at pleasing *practiced* ears and know how to delight *one another;* but, in composing for songs, the reigning taste seems to be quite out of nature or rather the reverse of nature, and yet, like a torrent, hurries them all away with it; one or two perhaps only excepted.

You, in the spirit of some ancient legislators, would influence the manners of your country by the united powers of poetry and music. By what I can learn of *their* songs, the music was simple, conformed itself to the usual pronunciation of words, as to measure, cadence or emphasis, etc., never disguised and confounded the language by making a long syllable short or a short one long when sung; their singing was only a more pleasing, because a melodious, manner of speaking; it was capable of all the graces of prose oratory, while it added the pleasure of harmony. A modern song, on the contrary, neglects all the proprieties and beauties of common speech, and in their place introduces its *defects* and *absurdities* as so many graces. I am afraid you will hardly take my word for this, and therefore I must endeavor to support it by proof. Here is the first song I lay my hand on. It happens to be a composition of one of our greatest masters, the ever-famous Handel. It is not one of his juvenile performances, before his taste could be improved and formed; it appeared when his reputation was at the highest, is greatly admired by all his admirers, and is really excellent in its kind. It is called, "The additional favorite Song in Judas Maccabeus*." Now I reckon among the defects and improprieties of common speech, the following, *viz.*

1. *Wrong placing of the accent or emphasis,* by laying it on words of no importance, or on wrong syllables.
2. *Drawling;* or extending the sound of words or syllables beyond their natural length.
3. *Stuttering;* or making many syllables of one.
4. *Unintelligibleness;* the result of the three foregoing united.
5. *Tautology;* and
6. *Screaming,* without cause.

For the *wrong placing of the accent, or emphasis,* see it on the word *their* instead of being on the word *vain.* And on the word *from,* and the wrong syllable *like.* For the *drawling,* see the last syllable of the word *wounded.* And in the syllable *wis,* and the word *from,* and syllable *bove.* For the stuttering, see the words *ne'er relieve.* Here are four syllables made of one and eight of three, but this is moderate. I have seen in another song, that I cannot now find, seventeen syllables made of three, and sixteen of one. The latter I remember was the word *charms; viz. cha, a, a, a, a, a, a, a, a, a, a, a, a, arms.* Stammering with a witness!

For the *unintelligibleness;* give this whole song to any

* Franklin included in his letter the music to the following lines: "with *their* vain my – ste – rious art.

God-*like* wisdom *from* a – bove.

Nor can heal the woun*ded* heart.

God-like *wis*dom *from* a – bove.

Ma – gic charms can *ne'er* re – *lieve* you."

taught singer and let her sing it to any company that have never heard it; you shall find they will not understand three words in ten. It is therefore, that at the oratorios and operas one sees with books in their hands all those who desire to understand what they hear sung by even our best performers.

For the *tautology;* you have, *with their vain mysterious art,* twice repeated; *magic charms can ne'er relieve you,* three times. *Nor can heal the wounded heart,* three times. *Godlike wisdom, from above,* twice; and, *this alone can ne'er deceive you,* two or three times. But this is reasonable when compared with *the Monster Polypheme, the Monster Polypheme,* a hundred times over and over, in his admired *Acis and Galatea.*

As to the *screaming;* perhaps I cannot find a fair instance in this song; but whoever has frequented our operas will remember many. And yet here methinks the words *no* and *e'er,* when sung to these notes, have a little of the air of *screaming,* and would actually be screamed by some singers.

I send you enclosed the song with its music at length. Read the words without the repetitions. Observe how few they are, and what a shower of notes attend them; you will then perhaps be inclined to think with me that, though the words might be the principal part of an ancient song, they are of small importance in a modern one; they are in short only a *pretence for singing.*

– From a letter to Peter Franklin
London, undated

DRESSING FOR THE TROPICS

Many decades before Europeans learned to wear light clothes in hot climates, Franklin showed by simple experiments the effect of the sun on clothing.

80

The different degrees of heat imbibed from the sun's rays by cloths of different colors, since I cannot find the notes of my experiment to send you, I must give it as well as I can from memory.

But first let me mention an experiment you may easily make yourself. Walk but a quarter of an hour in your garden when the sun shines, with a part of your dress white and a part black; then apply your hand to them alternately, and you will find a very great difference in their warmth. The black will be quite hot to the touch, the white still cool.

Another. Try to fire the paper with a burning glass. If it is white, you will not easily burn it; but if you bring the focus to a black spot, or upon letters written or printed, the paper will immediately be on fire under the letters.

Thus fullers and dyers find black cloths of equal thickness with white ones, and hung out equally wet, dry in the sun much sooner than the white, being more readily heated by the sun's rays. It is the same before a fire; the heat of which sooner penetrates black stockings than white ones, and so is apt sooner to burn a man's shins. Also beer much sooner warms in a black mug set before the fire than in a white one, or in a bright silver tankard.

My experiment was this. I took a number of little square pieces of broad cloth from a tailor's pattern card, of various colors. I laid them all out upon the snow in a bright sunshiny morning. In a few hours (I cannot now be exact as to the time) the black being warmed most by the sun was sunk so low as to be below the stroke of the sun's rays; the dark blue almost as low, the lighter blue not quite so much as the dark, the other colors less as they were lighter; and the quite white remained on the surface of the snow, not having entered it at all.

What signifies philosophy that does not apply to some use? May we not learn from hence that black clothes are not so fit to wear in a hot sunny climate or season as white ones; because in such clothes the body is more heated by the sun when we walk abroad, and are at the same time heated by the exercise, which double heat is apt to bring on putrid, dangerous fevers? That soldiers and seamen, who must march and labor in the sun, should in the East or West Indies have an uniform of white? That summer hats for men or women should be white, as repelling that heat which gives headaches to many, and to some the fatal stroke that the French call *coup de soleil?* That the ladies' summer hats, however, should be lined with black, as not reverberating on their faces those rays which are reflected upwards from the earth or water? That the putting a white cap of paper or linen *within* the crown of a black hat, as some do, will not keep out the heat, though it would if placed *without?* That fruit walls being blacked may receive so much heat from the sun in the daytime as to continue warm in some degree through the night, and thereby preserve the fruit from frosts, or forward its growth? – with sundry other particulars of less or greater importance that will occur from time to time to attentive minds?

> – From a letter to Mary Stevenson,
> London, August 10 1761

ON BAD SPELLING

English spelling exasperated Franklin. In 1768 he drew up his own reformed phonetic alphabet, adding several new characters. He never gave up hope of having it adopted, and almost twenty years later exchanged correspondence on the subject with Noah Webster, the great lexicographer, who had also worked out a reformed system. He wrote the following to his sister, Mrs. Jane Mecom.

You need not be concerned in writing to me about your bad spelling; for in my opinion, as our alphabet now stands, the bad spelling, or what is called so, is generally the best, as conforming to the sound of the letters and of the words. To give you an instance. A gentleman received a letter in which were these words – *Not finding Brown at hom, I delivered your meseg to his yf.* The gentleman finding it bad spelling, and therefore not very intelligible, called his lady to help him read it. Between them they picked out the meaning of all but the *yf*, which they could not understand. The lady proposed calling her chambermaid because Betty, she says, has the best knack at reading bad spelling of any one I know. Betty came, and was surprised that neither Sir nor Madam could tell what *yf* was.

"Why," says she, "yf spells *wife*; what else can it spell?"

And indeed, it is a much better, as well as shorter method of spelling *wife* than *doubleyou, i, ef, e,* which in reality spell *doubleyifey.*

– Philadelphia, July 4 1786

PETITION OF THE LETTER Z

To the Worshipful Isaac Bickerstaff, Esquire, Censor-General

The petition of the letter Z*, commonly called *Ezzard, Zed,* or *Izard,* most humbly showeth:

That your petitioner is of as high extraction, and has as good an estate as any other letter of the Alphabet;

---

* This is another of Franklin's jokes, illustrating his preoccupation with spelling. It purports to be an extract from the famous London weekly *Tatler,* founded in 1709 by Sir Richard Steele, who wrote for it under the name of Isaac Bickerstaff. In Franklin's reformed spelling, Z replaced S in Such words as "is," "as," and "was" and was used to form many plurals.

That there is therefore no reason why he should be treated as he is, with disrespect and indignity;

That he is not only actually placed at the tail of the Alphabet, when he had as much right as any other to be at the head; but is by the injustice of his enemies totally excluded from the word WISE; and his place injuriously filled by a little, hissing, crooked, serpentine, veneous letter called S, when it must be evident to your worship, and to all the world, that W,I,S,E, do not spell WIZE but WISE.

Your petitioner therefore prays that the Alphabet may by your censorial authority be reversed; and that in consideration of his long-suffering and patience he may be placed at the head of it; that S may be turned out of the word WISE; and the petitioner employed instead of him.

And your petitioner, as in duty bound, shall ever pray, etc. etc.

Mr. Bickerstaff, having examined the allegations of the above petition, judges and determines that Z be admonished to be content with his station, forbear reflections upon his brother letters, and remember his own small usefulness, and the little occasion there is for him in the Republic of Letters, since S whom he so despises can so well serve him instead.

– From *The Tatler*, No. 1778

PRESERVED IN MADEIRA

A retranslation of the French version made by the noted French scientist, Barbeu Dubourg, of Franklin's reply to his letter of April 15 1773.

Your observations on the causes of death, and the experiments which you propose for recalling to life those who appeared to be killed by lightning, demonstrate equally your sagacity and your humanity. It appears, that the doctrines of life and death in general are yet but little understood.

A toad buried in sand will live, it is said, till the sand becomes petrified, and then, being enclosed in the stone, it may still live for we know not how many ages. The facts which are cited in support of this opinion are too numerous and too circumstantial not to deserve a certain degree of credit. As we are accustomed to see all the animals with which we are acquainted eat and drink, it appears to us difficult to conceive how a toad can be supported in such a dungeon; but if we reflect that the necessity of nourishment which animals experience in their ordinary state proceeds from the continual waste of their substance by perspiration, it will appear less incredible that some animals in a torpid state, perspiring less because they use no exercise, should have less need of aliment, and that others, which are covered with scales or shells which stop perspiration, such as land- and sea-turtles, serpents, and some species of fish, should be able to subsist a considerable time without any nourishment whatever. A plant, with its flowers, fades and dies immediately if exposed to the air without having its root immersed in a humid soil, from which it may draw a sufficient quantity of moisture to supply that which exhales from its substance and is carried off continually by the air. Perhaps, however, if it were buried in quicksilver it might preserve for a considerable space of time its vegetable life, its smell, and color. If this be the case, it might prove a commodious method of transporting from distant countries those delicate plants which are unable to sustain the inclemency of the weather at sea, and which require particular care and attention.

I have seen an instance of common flies preserved in a manner somewhat similar. They had been drowned in Madeira wine, apparently about the time when it was bottled in Virginia to be sent hither (to London). At the opening of one of the bottles at the house of a friend where

I then was, three drowned flies fell into the first glass that was filled. Having heard it remarked that drowned flies were capable of being revived by the rays of the sun, I proposed making the experiment upon these. They were, therefore, exposed to the sun upon a sieve which had been employed to strain them out of the wine. In less than three hours two of them began by degrees to recover life. They commenced by some convulsive motions of the thighs, and at length they raised themselves upon their legs, wiped their eyes with their forefeet, beat and brushed their wings with their hind feet, and soon after began to fly, finding themselves in Old England without knowing how they came thither. The third continued lifeless till sunset, when losing all hopes of him, he was thrown away.

I wish it were possible, from this instance, to invent a method of embalming drowned persons in such a manner that they may be recalled to life at any period, however distant; for having a very ardent desire to see and observe the state of America a hundred years hence, I should prefer to any ordinary death the being immersed in a cask of Madeira wine with a few friends till that time, to be then recalled to life by the solar warmth of my dear country! But since in all probability we live in an age too early and too near the infancy of science to hope to see such an art brought in our time to its perfection, I must for the present content myself with the treat which you are so kind as to promise me of the resurrection of a fowl or a turkey-cock.

REFLECTIONS
ON THE SPIRIT OF INVENTION

There are everywhere a number of people who, being totally destitute of any inventive faculty themselves, do not readily conceive that others may possess it; they think of inventions as of miracles; there might be such formerly, but they are ceased. With these, everyone who offers a new invention is deemed a pretender; he had it from some other country, or from some book; a man of *their own acquaintance,* one who has no more sense than themselves, could not possibly, in their opinion, have been the inventor of anything. They are confirmed, too, in these sentiments by frequent instances of pretensions to invention which vanity is daily producing. That vanity, too, though an incitement to invention, is at the same time the pest of inventors. Jealousy and envy deny the merit or the novelty of your invention, but vanity, when the novelty and merit are established, claims it for its own. The smaller your invention is, the more mortification you receive in having the credit of it disputed with you by a rival, whom the jealousy and envy of others are ready to support against you, at least so far as to make the point doubtful. It is not in itself of importance enough for a dispute; no one would think your proofs and reasons worth their attention; and yet, if you do not dispute the point and demonstrate your right, you not only lose the credit of being in that instance *ingenious* but you suffer the disgrace of not being *ingenious;* not only of being a plagiary, but of being a plagiary for trifles. Had the invention been greater, it would have disgraced you less; for men have not so contemptible idea of him that robs for gold on the highway as of him that can pick pockets for half-pence and farthings. Thus through envy, jealousy, and the vanity of competitors for fame, the origin of many of the most extraordinary inventions, though produced within but a few centuries past, is involved in doubt and uncertainty. We scarce know to whom we are indebted for the *compass* and for *spectacles,* nor have even *paper* and *printing,* that record everything else, been able to preserve with certainty the name and reputation of their inventors. One would not, therefore, of all faculties or qualities of the mind, wish for a friend or a child that he should have that of invention. For his attempts to benefit mankind in that way, however well imagined, if they do not succeed, expose him, though very

unjustly, to general ridicule and contempt; and if they do
succeed to envy, robbery and abuse.

– From a letter to John Lining
Philadelphia, March 18 1775

IN FAVOR OF FRESH AIR

*Franklin's interest in science extended to medicine, and
although he had no medical training his detailed observations on the cause of the common cold attracted the attention of physicians. He repeated his then-radical views on
ventilation on several occasions; this passage comes from
a long essay on the cause and cure of smokey chimneys,
sent first to Jan Ingenhousz, the Dutch scientist, in Vienna,
and read to the American Philosophical Society on October 21 1785.*

I now look upon fresh air as a friend; I even sleep with
an open window. I am persuaded that no common air from
without is so unwholesome as the air within a close room
that has been often breathed and not changed. Moist air,
too, which formerly I thought pernicious, gives me now
no apprehensions, for considering that no dampness of air
applied to the outside of my skin can be equal to what is
applied to and touches it within, my whole body being full
of moisture, and finding that I can lie two hours in a bath
twice a week, covered with water, which certainly is much
damper than any air can be, and this for years together,
without catching cold or being in any other manner dis-
ordered by it, I no longer dread mere moisture, either in
air or in sheets or shirts; and I find it of importance to the
happiness of life, the being free from vain terrors, especially of objects that we are every day exposed inevitably
to meet with.

You physicians have of late happily discovered, after a contrary opinion had prevailed some ages, that fresh and cool air does good to persons in the smallpox and other fevers. It is to be hoped that in another century or two we may all find out that it is not bad even for people in health.

And, as to moist air, here I am at this present writing in a ship with above forty persons who have had no other but moist air to breathe for six weeks past; everything we touch is damp and nothing dries, yet we are all as healthy as we should be on the mountains of Switzerland, whose inhabitants are not more so than those of Bermuda or St. Helena, islands on whose rocks the waves are dashed into millions of particles, which fill the air with damp but produce no diseases, the moisture unmixed with the poisonous vapors arising from putrid marshes and stagnant pools, in which many insects die and corrupt the water.

These places only, in my opinion (which, however, I submit to yours) afford unwholesome air; and that it is not the mere water contained in damp air, but the volatile particles of corrupted animal matter mixed with that water which renders such air pernicious to those who breathe it. And I imagine it a cause of the same kind that renders the air in close rooms, where the perspirable matter is breathed over and over again by a number of assembled people, is hurtful to health. After being in such a situation, many find themselves affected by that *febricula* which the English alone call a *cold,* and perhaps from the name imagine that they caught the malady by *going out* of the room, when it was in fact by being in it. . . .

            – At sea, August 28 1785

ADVICE TO PASSENGERS

Franklin's eighth and last sea voyage returned him from Paris to Philadelphia at the age of seventy-nine. He occupied himself during the trip with detailed experiments and observations designed to improve the rigging of ships, prevent accidents, with remarks on navigation, the Gulf stream, the diet of sailors, the use of lifeboats, and many other matters. Written in the form of a letter to a French friend, the paper was read at a meeting of the American Philosophical Society in December, 1785, and published in Paris in 1787. In the following passage he turned his attention briefly to "trifles."

Some sailors may think the writer has given himself unnecessary trouble in pretending to advise them, for they have a little repugnance to the advice of landmen, whom they esteem ignorant and incapable of giving any worth notice, though it is certain that most of their instruments were the invention of landmen. At least the first vessel ever made to go on the water was certainly such. I will therefore add only a few words more, and they shall be addressed to passengers.

When you intend a long voyage, you may do well to keep your intention as much as possible a secret, or at least the time of your departure; otherwise you will be continually interrupted in your preparations by the visits of friends and acquaintance, who will not only rob you of the time you want, but put things out of your mind, so that when you come to sea you have the mortification to recollect points of business that ought to have been done, accounts you intended to settle, and conveniences you had proposed to bring with you, etc., all which have been omitted through the effect of these officious friendly visits. Would it not be well if this custom could be changed; if the voyager, after having, without interruption, made all his preparations, should use some of the time he has left in going himself to take leave of his friends at their own houses, and let them come to congratulate him on his happy return?

It is not always in your power to make a choice in your

captain, though much of your comfort in the passage may depend on his personal character, as you must for so long a time be confined to his company, and under his direction; if he be a sensible, sociable, good-natured, obliging man, you will be so much the happier. Such there are; but if he happens to be otherwise, and is only skilful, careful, watchful, and active in the conduct of his ship, excuse the rest, for these are the essentials.

Whatever right you may have by agreement in the mass of stores laid in by him for the passengers, it is good to have some particular things in your own possession, so as to be always at your own command.

1. Good water, that of the ship being often bad. You can be sure of having it good only by bottling it from a clear spring or well, and in clean bottles. 2. Good tea. 3. Coffee, ground. 4. Chocolate. 5. Wine of the sort you particularly like, and cider. 6. Raisins. 7. Almonds. 8. Sugar, 9. Capillaire. 10. Lemons. 11. Jamaica spirits. 12. Eggs, greased. 13. Diet bread. 14. Portable soup. 15. Rusks. As to fowls, it is not worth while to have any called yours, unless you could have the feeding and managing of them according to your own judgment, under your own eye. As they are generally treated at present in ships, they are for the most part sick, and their flesh tough and hard as whitleather. All seamen have an opinion, broached, I suppose, at first prudently, for saving of water when short, that fowls do not know when they have drunk enough and will kill themselves if you give them too much, so they are served with a little only once in two days. This is poured into troughs that lie sloping, and therefore immediately runs down to the lower end. There the fowls ride upon one another's back to get at it, and some are not happy enough to reach and once dip their bills in it. Thus tantalized, and tormented with thirst, they cannot digest their dry food, they fret, pine, sicken and die. Some are found dead, and thrown overboard every morning, and those killed for the table are not eatable. Their troughs

should be in little divisions, like cups, to hold the water separately. But this is never done. The sheep and hogs are therefore your best dependence for fresh meat at sea, the mutton being generally tolerable and the pork excellent.

It is possible your captain may have provided so well in the general stores, as to render some of the particulars above recommended of little or no use to you. But there are frequently in the ship poorer passengers, who are taken at a lower price, lodge in the steerage, and have no claim to any of the cabin provisions, or to any but those kinds that are allowed the sailors. These people are sometimes dejected, sometimes sick; there may be women and children among them. In a situation where there is no going to market to purchase such necessaries, a few of these your superfluities, distributed occasionally, may be of great service, restore health, save life, make the miserable happy, and thereby afford you infinite pleasure.

The worst thing in ordinary merchant ships is the cookery. They have no professed cook, and the worst hand as a seaman is appointed to that office, in which he is not only very ignorant but very dirty. The sailors have therefore a saying, that *God sends meat, and the Devil cooks.* Passengers more piously disposed, and willing to believe Heaven orders all things for the best, may suppose that, knowing the sea air and constant exercise by the motion of the vessel would give us extraordinary appetites, bad cooks were kindly sent to prevent our eating too much; or that, foreseeing we should have bad cooks, good appetites were furnished to prevent our starving. If you cannot trust to these circumstances, a spirit-lamp with a blaze-pan may enable you to cook some little things for yourself; such as a hash, a soup, etc. And it might be well also to have among your stores some potted meats which, if well put up, will keep long good. A small tin oven, to place with the open side before the fire, may be another good utensil, in which your own servant may roast for you a bit of pork or mutton. You will sometimes be induced to eat of the ship's salt beef, as it is often good. You will find cider the best quencher of that thirst which salt meat or fish occasions. The ship biscuit is too hard for some sets of teeth. It may be softened by toasting. But rusk is better for being made of good fermented bread, sliced and baked a second time, the pieces imbibe the water easily, soften immediately, digest more kindly, and are therefore more wholesome than the unfermented biscuit. By the way, rusk is the true original biscuit, so prepared to keep for sea, biscuit in French signifying *twice baked*. If your dry peas boil hard, a two pound iron shot put with them into the pot will, by the motion of the ship, grind them as fine as mustard.

The accidents I have seen at sea with large dishes of soup upon a table, from the motion of the ship, have made me wish that our potters or pewterers would ma... soup dishes in divisions, like a set of small bowls united together, each containing about sufficient for one person for then, when the ship should make a sudden heel, the soup would not in a body flow over one side, and fall into people's laps and scald them, as is sometimes the case, but would be retained in the separate divisions....

> – From *Maritime Observations,*
> At sea, on board the London packet,
> *Captain Truxton*
> August, 1785

daughter; for with my consent and approbation he married soon after I left England a very agreeable West India lady with whom he is very happy. I accompanied him to his government*, where he met with the kindest reception from the people of all ranks, and has lived with them ever since in the greatest harmony. A river only parts that province and ours, and his residence is within seventeen miles of me, so that we frequently see each other.

In the spring of 1763, I set out on a tour through all the northern colonies to inspect and regulate the post-offices in the several provinces**. In this journey I spent the summer, traveled about sixteen hundred miles and did not get home till the beginning of November. The Assembly sitting through the following winter, and warm disputes arising between them and the governor, I became wholly engaged in public affairs; for besides my duty as an Assemblyman, I had another trust to execute, that of being one of the commissioners appointed by law to dispose of the public money appropriated to the raising and paying an army to act against the Indians and defend the frontiers.

And then, in December, we had two insurrections of the back inhabitants of our province, by whom twenty poor Indians were murdered that had, from the first settlement of the province lived among us, under the protection of our government. This gave me a good deal of employment; for as the rioters threatened further mischief, and their actions seemed to be approved by an ever-acting party, I wrote a pamphlet entitled *A Narrative, etc****. (which I think I sent you) to strengthen the hands of our weak government by rendering the proceedings of the

* William Franklin had been appointed governor of New Jersey.
** Franklin had been appointed postmaster-general for the American colonies in 1753.
*** *A Narrative of the Late Massacres in Lancaster County,* see page 58

rioters unpopular and odious. This had a good effect; and afterwards, when a great body of them with arms marched towards the capital in defiance of the government, with an avowed resolution to put to death one hundred and forty Indian converts then under its protection, I formed an Association at the governor's request, for his and their defence, we having no militia. Near one thousand of the citizens accordingly took arms; Governor Penn made my house for some time his headquarters and did everything by my advice; so that for about forty-eight hours I was a very great man; as I had been once some years before, in a time of public danger*.

But the fighting face we put on, and the reasoning we used with the insurgents (for I went at the request of the governor and the council with three others to meet and discourse with them) having turned them back and restored quiet to the city, I became a less man than ever; for I had, by this transaction, made myself many enemies among the populace; and the governor (with whose family our public disputes had long placed me in an unfriendly light, and the services I had lately rendered him not being of the kind that make a man acceptable) thinking it a favorable opportunity, joined the whole weight of the proprietary interest to get me out of the Assembly; which was accordingly effected at the last election by a majority of about twenty-five in four thousand voters.

The House, however, when they met in October, approved of the resolutions taken while I was Speaker, of petitioning the crown for a change of government, and requested me to return to England to prosecute that petition; which service I accordingly undertook and embarked at the beginning of November last, being accompanied to the ship, sixteen miles, by a cavalcade of three hundred

* In 1747–48 Franklin organized a volunteer militia of 10 000 men to protect Pennsylvania from an anticipated attack by French and Spanish privateers (England was at war with both countries).

of my friends, who filled our sails with their good wishes, and I arrived in thirty days at London.

Here I have been ever since, engaged in that and other public affairs relating to America, which are like to continue some time longer upon my hands; but I promise you that when I am quit of these I will engage in no other; and that, as soon as I have recovered the ease and leisure I hope for, the task you require of me, of finishing my Art of Virtue, shall be performed. In the meantime I must request you would excuse me on this consideration, that the powers of the mind are possessed by different men in different degrees, and that everyone cannot, like Lord Kames*, intermix literary pursuits and important business without prejudice to either.

– Letter to Lord Kames,
London, June 2 1765

PLAN FOR UNION WITH BRITAIN

Almost until the outbreak of hostilities, Franklin hoped to be able to bring about a peaceful solution of the conflict with Britain. His views and his diminishing optimism are well represented in this letter to his friend Lord Kames, who he hoped would become a spokesman for these opinions: A union in which the colonies would be permitted to run their own internal affairs, subject only to the King, and having representation in Parliament.

I am fully persuaded with you that a *consolidating union* by a fair and equal representation of all the parts of this empire in Parliament is the only firm basis on which its political grandeur and prosperity can be founded. Ireland once wished it, but now rejects it. The time has been when

* Distinguished Scottish Judge and man of letters

the colonies might have been pleased with it; they are now *indifferent* about it; and if it is much longer delayed they too will *refuse* it. But the pride of this people cannot bear the thought of it, and therefore it will be delayed. Every man in England seems to consider himself as a piece of a sovereign over America; seems to jostle himself into the throne with the King, and talks of *our subjects in the colonies*. The Parliament cannot well and wisely make laws suited to the colonies without being properly and truly informed of their circumstances, abilities, temper, etc. This it cannot be without representatives from thence. . . .

It is a common but mistaken notion here that the colonies were planted at the expense of Parliament, and that therefore the Parliament has a right to tax them, etc. The truth is, they were planted at the expense of private adventurers who went over there to settle, with leave of the King, given by charter. On receiving this leave and those charters, the adventurers voluntarily engaged to remain the King's subjects, though in a foreign country; a country which had not been conquered by either King or Parliament, but was possessed by a free people.

When our planters arrived, they purchased the lands of the natives, without putting King or Parliament to any expense. Parliament had no hand in their settlement, was never so much as consulted about their constitution, and took no kind of notice of them till many years after they were established. . . Thus all the colonies acknowledge the King as their sovereign; his governors there represent his person; laws are made by their Assemblies or little parliaments with the governor's assent, subject still to the King's pleasure to affirm or annul them. Suits arising in the colonies and between colony and colony, are determined by the King in Council. In this view, they seem so many separate little states, subject to the same prince. The sovereignty of the King is therefore easily understood. But nothing is more common here than to talk of the *sovereignty* of Parliament, and the sovereignty of this nation over the colonies; a kind of sovereignty the idea of which is not so clear, nor does it clearly appear on what foundation it is established. . . .

Upon the whole, I have lived so great a part of my life in Britain, and have formed so many friendships in it, that I love it and sincerely wish it prosperity; and therefore wish to see that union on which alone I think it can be secured and established. As to America, the advantages of such a union to her are not so apparent. She may suffer at present under the arbitrary power of this country; she may suffer for a while in a separation from it; but these are temporary evils which she will outgrow.

Scotland and Ireland are differently circumstanced. Confined by the sea, they can scarcely increase in numbers, wealth and strength so as to overbalance England. But America, an immense territory, favored by nature with all advantages of climate, soils, great navigable rivers, lakes, etc., must become a great country, populous and mighty; and will, in a less time than is generally conceived, be able to shake off any shackles that may be imposed upon her, and perhaps place them on the imposers.

In the meantime, every act of oppression will sour their tempers, lessen greatly if not annihilate, the profits of your commerce with them, and hasten their final revolt; for the seeds of liberty are universally found there, and nothing can eradicate them. And yet there remains among that people so much respect, veneration and affection for Britain that, if cultivated prudently, with a kind usage and tenderness for their privileges, they might be easily governed still for ages without force or any considerable expense. But I do not see here a sufficient quantity of the wisdom that is necessary to produce such a conduct, and I lament the want of it. . . .

– London, April 11 1767

I took the resolution of making a trip with Sir John Pringle* into France. We set out on the 28th past. All the way to Dover we were furnished with postchaises, hung so as to lean forward, the top coming down over one's eyes like a hood, as if to prevent one's seeing the country; which being one of my great pleasures, I was engaged in perpetual disputes with the innkeepers, ostlers, and postilions about getting the straps taken up a hole or two before, and let down as much behind, they insisting that the chaise leaning forward was an ease to the horses, and that the contrary would kill them. I suppose the chaise leaning forward looks to them like a willingness to go forward, and that its hanging back shows reluctance. They added other reasons, that were no reasons at all, and made me, as upon a hundred other occasions, almost wish that mankind had never been endowed with a reasoning faculty, since they know so little how to make use of it, and so often mislead themselves by it, and that they had been furnished with a good sensible instinct instead of it.

At Dover the next morning we embarked for Calais with a number of passengers who had never before been at sea. They would previously make a hearty breakfast because, if the wind should fail, we might not get over till supper time. Doubtless they thought that when they had paid for their breakfast they had a right to it, and that when they had swallowed it they were sure of it. But they had scarce been out half an hour before the sea laid claim to it, and they were obliged to deliver it up. So that it seems there are uncertainties, even beyond those between the cup and the lip. If ever you go to sea, take my advice, and live sparingly a day or two beforehand. The sickness, if any, will be lighter and sooner over. . .

Various impositions we suffered from boatmen, porters,

* Sir John Pringle was physician to the British Queen.

and the like, on both sides the water. I know not which are most rapacious, the English or French, but the latter have, with their knavery, most politeness.

The roads we found equally good with ours in England, in some places paved with smooth stones, like our new streets, for many miles together, and rows of trees on each side, and yet there are no turnpikes. But then the poor peasants complained to us grievously that they were o-bliged to work upon the roads full two months in the year, without being paid for their labor. Whether this is truth or whether, like Englishmen, they grumble, cause or no cause, I have not yet been able fully to inform myself.

The women we saw at Calais, on the road, at Boulogne, and in the inns and villages, were generally of dark complexions; but arriving at Abbeville we found a sudden change, a multitude of both women and men in that place appearing remarkably fair. Whether this is owing to a small colony of spinners, woolcombers, and weavers, brought hither from Holland with the woolen manufac-tory about sixty years ago, or to their being less exposed to the sun than in other places, their business keeping them much within doors, I know not. Perhaps, as in some other cases, different causes may club in producing the effect, but the effect itself is certain. Never was I in a place of greater industry, wheels and looms going in every house.

As soon as we left Abbeville, the swarthiness returned. I speak generally; for here are some fair women at Paris who, I think, are not whitened by art. As to rouge, they don't pretend to imitate nature in laying it on. There is no gradual diminution of the color, from the full bloom in the middle of the cheek to the faint tint near the sides, nor does it show itself differently in different faces. I have not had the honor of being at any lady's toilette to see how it is laid on, but I fancy I can tell you how it is or may be done. Cut a hole of three inches diameter in a piece of paper; place it on the side of your face in such a manner as that the top of the hole may be just under the eye; then, with a brush dipped in the color, paint face and paper together so when the paper is taken off there will remain a round patch of red exactly the form of the hole. This is the mode, from the actresses on the stage upwards through all ranks of ladies to the princesses of the blood; but it stops there, the Queen not using it, having in the serenity, complacence, and benignity, that shine so eminently in, or rather through her countenance, sufficient beauty, though now an old woman, to do extremely well without it.

You see I speak of the Queen as if I had seen her; and so I have, for you must know I have been at court. We went to Versailles last Sunday, and had the honor of being presented to the King*; he spoke to both of us very graciously and very cheerfully, is a handsome man, has a very lively look, and appears younger than he is. In the evening we were at the *Grand Couvert,* where the family sup in public. The table was half a hollow square, the servi gold. When either made a sign for drink, the word was given by one of the waiters; *À boire pour le Roi, or À boire pour la Reine**.* Then two persons came from within, the one with wine and the other with water in *carafes;* each drank a little glass of what he brought, and then put both the *carafes* with a glass on a salver, and then presented it. Their distance from each other was such as that other chairs might have been placed between any two of them. An officer of the court brought us up through the crowd of spectators, and placed Sir John so as to stand between the Queen and Madame Victoire. The King talked a good deal to Sir John, asking many questions about our royal family; and did me too the honor of taking some notice of me. . . .

Versailles has had infinite sums laid out in building it and supplying it with water. Some say the expenses exceeded eighty millions sterling. The range of buildings is

---

* Louis XV
** "A drink for the King" or "A drink for the Queen."

immense; the garden-front most magnificent, all of hewn stone; the number of statues, figures, urns, etc., in marble and bronze of exquisite workmanship, is beyond conception. But the waterworks are out of repair, and so is a great part of the front next the town, looking with its shabby, half-brick walls, and broken windows, not much better than the houses in Durham Yard.

There is, in short, both at Versailles and Paris a prodigious mixture of magnificence and negligence, with every kind of elegance except that of cleanliness, and what we call tidiness. Though I must do Paris the justice to say that in two points of cleanliness they exceed us. The water they drink, though from the river, they render as pure as that of the best spring by filtering it through cisterns filled with sand; and the streets with constant sweeping are fit to walk in, though there is no paved footpath. Accordingly, many well dressed people are constantly seen walking in them. The crowd of coaches and chairs for this reason is not so great. Men as well as women carry umbrellas in their hands, which they extend in case of rain or too much sun; and a man with an umbrella not taking up more than three foot square, or nine square feet of the street, when if in a coach he would take up two hundred and forty square feet, you can easily conceive that though the streets here are narrow, they may be much less encumbered. They are extremely well paved; the stones, being generally cubes, when worn on one side, may be turned and become new.

The civilities we everywhere receive give us the strongest impressions of the French politeness. It seems to be a point settled here universally that strangers are to be treated with respect, and one has just the same deference shown one here by being a stranger as in England by being a lady. The custom-house officers at Port St. Denis, as we entered Paris, were about to seize two dozen of excellent Bordeaux wine given us at Boulogne and which we brought with us, but, as soon as they found we were strangers it was immediately remitted on that account. At the Church of Notre Dame, where we went to see a magnificent illumination, with figures, etc. for the deceased Dauphiness, we found an immense crowd who were kept out by guards; but the officer being told that we were strangers from England, he immediately admitted us, accompanied and showed us everything. Why don't we practice this urbanity to Frenchmen? Why should they be allowed to outdo us in any thing?

Here is an exhibition of painting, like ours in London, to which multitudes flock daily. I am not connoisseur enough to judge which has most merit. Every night, Sundays not excepted, here are plays or operas; and though the weather has been hot, and the houses full, one is not incommoded by the heat so much as with us in winter. They must have some way of changing the air that we are not acquainted with. I shall inquire into it.

Traveling is one way of lengthening life, at least in appearance. It is but about a fortnight since we left London, but the variety of scenes we have gone through makes it seem equal to six months living in one place. Perhaps I have suffered a greater change, too, in my own person, than I could have done in six years at home. I had not been here six days before my tailor and *perruquier* had transformed me into a Frenchman. Only think what a figure I make in a little bag-wig and with naked ears! They told me I was become twenty years younger, and looked very gallant.

This letter shall cost you a shilling, and you may consider it cheap, when you reflect that it has cost me at least fifty guineas to get into the situation that enables me to write it. Besides, I might, if I had stayed at home, have won perhaps two shillings of you at cribbage. By the way, now I mention cards, let me tell you that quadrille is now out of fashion here, and English whist all the mode at Paris and the court.

– From a letter to Mary Stevenson
Paris, September 14 1767

NOTE
RESPECTING TRADE AND MANUFACTURE

Suppose a country, X, with three manufactures, as *cloth*, *silk*, *iron*, supplying three other countries, A, B, C, but is desirous of increasing the vent and raising the price of cloth in favor of her own clothiers.

In order to do this, she forbids the importation of foreign cloth from A.

A, in return, forbids silks from X.

Then the silk-workers complain of a decay of trade.

And X, to content them, forbids silks from B.

B, in return, forbids iron ware from X.

Then the iron-workers complain of decay.

And X forbids the importation of iron from C.

C, in return, forbids cloth from X.

What is got by all these prohibitions?

Answer: All four find their common stock of the enjoyments and conveniences of life diminished.

London, July 7 1767

CORRUPTION IN PARLIAMENT

At the time of King George III, only three Englishmen in a hundred had a right to vote, and a handful of voters could elect a majority in Parliament. The King and the landed aristocracy controlled the elections, using appointments and national funds for bribery.

The Parliament have of late been acting an egregious farce, calling before them the mayor and aldermen of Oxford for proposing a sum to be paid by their old members on being rechosen at the next election; and sundry printers and brokers for advertising and dealing in boroughs, etc.

107

The Oxford people were sent to Newgate, and discharged after some days on humble petition and receiving the Speaker's reprimand upon their knees. The House could scarcely keep countenances, knowing as they all do that the practice is general. People say they mean nothing more than to *beat down the price* by a little discouragement of borough jobbing, now that their own elections are coming on. The price indeed is grown exorbitant, no less than *four thousand pounds* for a member.

Mr. Beckford has brought in a bill for preventing bribery and corruption in elections, wherein was a clause to oblige every member to swear, on his admission into the House, that he had not directly or indirectly given any bribe to any elector; but this was so universally exclaimed against as answering no purpose but perjuring the members, that he has been obliged to withdraw the clause. It was indeed a cruel contrivance of his, worse than the gunpowder plot; for that was only to blow the Parliament up to heaven, this to sink them all down to – – – –.

Mr. Thurlow opposed his bill by a long speech. Beckford, in reply, gave a dry hit to the House that is repeated everywhere.

"The honorable gentleman," says he, "in his learned discourse, gave us first one definition of corruption, then he gave us another definition of corruption, and I think he was about to give us a third. Pray does that gentleman imagine *there is any member of this House that* does not KNOW what corruption is?"

Which occasioned only a roar of laughter, for they are so hardened in the practice, that they are very little ashamed of it.

– From a letter to Joseph Galloway*
London, February 17 1768

* Speaker of the Pennsylvania Assembly

AN INTERVIEW
WITH LORD HILLSBOROUGH

As agent in London for Pennsylvania, Georgia, New Jersey and Massachusetts, Franklin went to pay his respects to Lord Hillsborough, British Secretary of State for America. He sent the following dramatization of the meeting to Samuel Cooper of the Massachusetts House of Representatives, adding: "I have since heard that his lordship took great offence at some of my last words, which he calls extremely rude and abusive. He assured a friend of mine that they were equivalent to telling him to his face that the colonies could expect neither favor nor justice during his administration. I find he did not mistake me." Franklin's influence played a part in the removal of Lord Hillsborough from office the following year.

Wednesday, January 16 1771

I went this morning to wait on Lord Hillsborough. The porter at first denied His Lordship, on which I left my name and drove off. But before the coach got out of the square, the coachman heard a call, turned, and went back to the door, when the porter came and said: "His Lordship will see you, Sir."

I was shown into the levee room, where I found Governor Bernard, who I understand attends there constantly. Several other gentlemen were there attending, with whom I sat down a few minutes, when Secretary Pownall came out to us, and said his Lordship desired I would come in.

I was pleased with this ready admission and preference, having sometimes waited three or four hours for my turn; and, being pleased, I could more easily put on the open, cheerful countenance that my friends advised me to wear. His Lordship came towards me, and said:

"I was dressing in order to go to Court; but hearing that

you were at the door, who are a man of business, I determined to see you immediately."

I thanked his Lordship, and said that my business at present was not much; it was only to pay my respects to His Lordship and to acquaint him with my appointment by the House of Representatives of Massachusetts Bay to be their agent here, in which station if I could be of any service – I was going on to say "to the public I should be very happy"; but his Lordship, whose countenance changed at my naming that province, cut me short by saying with something between a smile and a sneer:

L. H. I must set you right there, Mr. Franklin, you are not agent.

B. F. Why, my Lord?

L. H. You are not appointed.

B. F. I do not understand your Lordship; I have the appointment in my pocket.

L. H. You are mistaken; I have later and better advices. I have a letter from Governor Hutchinson; he would not give his assent to the bill.

B. F. There was no bill, my Lord; it was a vote of the House.

L. H. There was a bill presented to the governor for the purpose of appointing you and another, one Dr. Lee, I think he is called, to which the governor refused his assent.

B. F. I cannot understand this, my Lord; I think there must be some mistake in it. Is your Lordship quite sure that you have such a letter?

L. H. I will convince you of it directly. *(Rings the bell.)* Mr. Pownall will come in and satisfy you.

B. F. It is not necessary that I should now detain your Lordship from dressing. You are going to Court. I will wait on your Lordship another time.

L. H. No, stay; he will come immediately. *(To the servant.)* Tell Mr. Pownall I want him. *(Mr. Pownall comes in.)*

L. H. Have not you at hand Governor Hutchinson's letter mentioning his refusing his assent to the bill for appointing Dr. Franklin agent?

Sec. P. My Lord?

L. H. Is there not such a letter?

Sec. P. No, my Lord; there is a letter relating to some bill for the payment of a salary to Mr. De Berdt, and I think to some other agent, to which the governor had refused his assent.

L. H. And is there nothing in the letter to the purpose I mention?

Sec. P. No, my Lord.

B. F. I thought it could not well be, my Lord; as my letters are by the last ships, and they mention no such thing. Here is the authentic copy of the vote of the House appointing me, in which there is no mention of any act intended. Will your Lordship please to look at it? *(With seeming unwillingness he takes it, but does not look into it.)*

L. H. An information of this kind is not properly brought to me as Secretary of State. The Board of Trade is the proper place.

B. F. I will leave the paper then with Mr. Pownall to be –

L. H. (Hastily) To what end would you leave it with him?

B. F. To be entered on the minutes of that Board, as usual.

L. H. (Angrily) It shall not be entered there. No such paper shall be entered there while I have anything to do with the business of that Board. The House of Representatives has no right to appoint an agent. We shall take no notice of any agents but such as are appointed by acts of Assembly, to which the governor gives his assent. We have had confusion enough already. Here is one agent appointed by the Council, another by the House of Representatives. Which of these is agent for the province? Who are we to hear in provincial affairs? An agent appointed by act of Assembly we can understand. No other will be attended to for the future, I can assure you.

B. F. I cannot conceive, my Lord, why the consent of the governor should be thought necessary to the appointment of an agent for the people. It seems to me that –

L. H. (With a mixed look of anger and contempt) I shall not enter into a dispute with *you,* Sir, upon this subject.

B. F. I beg your Lordship's pardon; I do not presume to dispute with your Lordship. I would only say that it seems to me that every body of men who cannot appear in person where business relating to them may be transacted, should have a right to appear by an agent. The concurrence of the governor does not seem to be necessary. It is the business of the people that is to be done; he is not one of them; he is himself an agent.

L. H. (Hastily) Whose agent is he?

B. F. The King's, my Lord.

L. H. No such matter. He is one of the corporation by the province charter. No agent can be appointed but by an act, nor any act pass without his assent. Besides, this proceeding is directly contrary to express instructions.

B. F. I did not know there had been such instructions. I am not concerned in any offence against them, and –

L. H. Yes, your offering such a paper to be entered is an offence against them *(Folding it up again without having read a word of it.)* No such appointment shall be entered. When I came into the administration of American affairs I found them in great disorder. By *my firmness* they are now something mended; and while I have the honor to hold the seals I shall continue the same conduct, the same *firmness.* I think my duty to the master I serve, and to the government of this nation, requires it of me. If that conduct is not approved, *they* may take my office from me when they please. I shall make them a bow, and thank them; I shall resign with pleasure. That gentleman knows

it (pointing to Mr. Pownall); but while I continue in it
I shall resolutely persevere in the same *firmness*. (*Spoken
with great warmth, and turning pale in his discourse, as
if he was angry at something or somebody besides the
agent, and of more consequence to himself.*)

B. F.   (*Reaching out his hand for the paper, which his
Lordship returned to him*) I beg your Lordship's pardon
for taking up so much of your time. It is, I believe, of no
great importance whether the appointment is acknowledged or not, for I have not the least conception that an
agent can *at present* be of any use to any of the Colonies.
I shall therefore give your Lordship no further trouble.
(*Withdrew.*)

HOW TO MAINTAIN AN EMPIRE

*The following "Rules" and the next in sequence, its com-
panion piece, "An Edict of the King of Prussia," were
written by Franklin in the autumn of 1773 for the London
"Public Advertiser" to expose, as he explained to his son,
"the conduct of this country towards the colonies in a short,
comprehensive and striking view, and stated therefore in
out-of-the-way forms, as most likely to take the general
attention."*

*The first proved not only timely but timeless, and was
reprinted as a pamphlet twenty-six years later in London
in order to meet a steady public demand, although the
actual grievances referred to were then ancient history.
The second was one of the most successful of the hoaxes
and parodies in which Franklin delighted, and sold out
the first day. In it the German ruler is made to impose
on Britain the restrictions on trade and manufacture which
Britain was actually enforcing against her colonies. Of
the public's reaction Franklin wrote: "What made it more
noticed here was that people in reading it were, as the
phrase is, taken in, till they had got half through it, and*

imagined it as a real edict, to which mistake I suppose the King of Prussia's character must have contributed."

RULES FOR REDUCING
A GREAT EMPIRE TO A SMALL ONE

An ancient sage valued himself upon this, that though he could not fiddle, he knew how to make a great city of a little one. The science that I, a modern simpleton, am about to communicate, is the very reverse.

I address myself to all ministers who have the management of extensive dominions which from their very greatness have been troublesome to govern because the multiplicity of their affairs leaves no time for fiddling.

1. In the first place, Gentlemen, you are to consider that a great empire, like a great cake, is most easily diminished at the edges. Turn your attention, therefore, first to your *remotest* provinces; that as you get rid of them the next may follow in order.

2. That the possibility of this separation may always exist, take special care the provinces are *never incorporated with the mother country*; that they do not enjoy the same common rights, the same privileges in commerce; and that they are governed by severer laws, all of your enacting, without allowing them any share in the choice of legislators. By carefully making and preserving such distinctions, you will (to keep my simile of the cake) act like a wise gingerbread-baker who, to facilitate a division, cuts his dough half through in those places where, when baked, he would have it broken to pieces.

3. Those remote provinces have perhaps been acquired, purchased or conquered at the sole expense of the settlers or their ancestors; without the aid of the mother country. If this could happen to increase her strength

by their growing numbers, ready to join in her wars; her commerce by their growing demand for her manufactures; or her naval power by greater employment for her ships and seamen, they may probably suppose some merit in this, and that it entitles them to some favor; you are therefore to *forget it all, or resent it,* as if they had done you an injury. If they happen to be zealous whigs, friends of liberty, nurtured in revolution principles, remember all that to their prejudice and contrive to punish it. . . .

4. However peaceably your colonies have submitted to your government, shown their affection to your interests, and patiently borne their grievances; you are to suppose them *always inclined to revolt* and treat them accordingly. Quarter troops among them, who by their insolence may provoke the rising of mobs and by their bullets and bayonets suppress them. By this means, like the husband who uses his wife ill from suspicion, you may in time convert your suspicions into realities.

5. Remote provinces must have governors and judges to represent the royal person and execute everywhere the delegated parts of his office and authority... You are therefore to be careful whom you recommend to those offices. If you can find prodigals who have ruined their fortunes, broken gamesters or stockjobbers, these may do well as governors; for they will probably be rapacious and provoke the people by their extortions. Wrangling proctors and pettifogging lawyers, too, are not amiss... If withal they should be ignorant, wrongheaded and insolent, so much the better.

6. To confirm these impressions and strike them deeper, whenever the injured come to the capital with complaints of mal-administration, oppression or injustice, *punish such suitors* with long delay, enormous expense, and a final judgment in favor of the oppressor. This will have an admirable effect every way. . . .

7. When such governors have crammed their coffers and made themselves so odious to the people that they can no longer remain among them with safety to their persons, *recall and reward* them with pensions. . . .

8. . . . *Despise* (your colonies') *voluntary grants* and resolve to harass them with *novel taxes*. They will probably complain to your Parliament that they are taxed by a body in which they have no representative, and that this is contrary to common right. They will petition for redress. Let the Parliament flout their claims, reject their petitions, refuse even to suffer the reading of them, and treat the petitioners with the utmost contempt. . . .

9. In laying these taxes, never regard the heavy burdens those remote people already undergo in defending their own frontiers, supporting their own provincial government, making new roads, building bridges. . . Forget the restraint you lay on their trade for your own benefit, and the advantage a monopoly of this trade gives your exacting merchants . . . But remember to make your arbitrary tax more grievous to your province by public declarations importing that your power of taxing them has *no limits;* so that when you take from them without their consent a shilling in the pound you have a clear right to the other nineteen. . . .

10. Possibly, indeed, some of them might still comfort themselves and say, "Though we have no property, we have yet something left that is valuable; we have constitutional *liberty, both of person and of conscience. . .* To annihilate this comfort, begin by laws to perplex their commerce with infinite regulations, impossible to be remembered and observed; ordain seizures of their property for every failure; take away the trial of such property by jury and give it to arbitrary judges of your own appointing, and of the lowest characters in

the country... Then let there be a formal declaration of both Houses that opposition to your edicts is treason, and that persons suspected of treason in the provinces may, according to some obsolete law, be seized and sent to the metropolis of the empire for trial....

11. To make your taxes more odious and more likely to procure resistance, send from the capital a *board of officers* to superintend the collection, *composed of the most indiscreet,* ill-bred and insolent you can find. Let these have large salaries out of the extorted revenue, and live in open, grating luxury upon the sweat and blood of the industrious; whom they are to worry continually with groundless and expensive prosecutions before the above-mentioned arbitrary revenue judges; all at the cost of the party prosecuted....

16. If you are told of *discontents* in your colonies, never believe that they are general or that you have given occasion for them; therefore do not think of applying any remedy or of changing any offensive measure. Redress no grievance lest they should be encouraged to demand the redress of some other grievance... Suppose all *their* complaints to be invented and promoted by a few factious demagogues whom if you could catch and hang, all would be quiet. Catch and hang a few of them accordingly; and the blood of the martyrs shall work miracles in favor of your purpose....

20. Lastly, invest the *general of your army in the provinces* with great and unconstitutional powers, and free him from the control of even your own civil governors. Let him have troops enough under his command, with all the fortresses in his possession; and who knows but (like some provincial generals in the Roman empire, and encouraged by the universal discontent you have produced) he may take it into his head to set up for himself? If he should, and you have carefully practiced the few excellent rules of mine, take my word for it,

all the provinces will immediately join him; and you will that day (if you have not done it sooner) get rid of the trouble of governing them, and all the plagues attending their commerce and connection from thenceforth and for ever.

– London, September 1773

AN EDICT BY THE KING OF PRUSSIA

Danzig, September 5 1773

We have long wondered here at the supineness of the English nation under the Prussian impositions upon its trade entering our port. We did not, till lately, know the claims, ancient and modern, that hang over that nation; and therefore could not suspect that it might submit to those impositions from a sense of duty or from principles of equity. The following Edict, just made public, may, if serious, throw some light upon this matter.

"FREDERIC, by the grace of God, King of Prussia, etc., etc., etc. to all present and to come, *(à tous les présents et à venir)* health. The peace now enjoyed throughout our dominions, having afforded us leisure to apply ourselves to the regulation of commerce, the improvement of our finances, and at the same time the easing our *domestic* subjects in their taxes; for these causes, and other good considerations us thereunto moving, we hereby make known that, after having deliberated these affairs in our Council, present our dear brothers, and other great officers of the state, members of the same; we, of our certain knowledge, full power, and authority royal, have made and issued this present Edict, *viz.*

"Whereas it is well known to all the world, that Britain were by colonies of people subject to our renowned ducal ancestors, and drawn from their dominions, under the conduct of Hengist, Horsa, Hella, Uffa, Cerdicus, Ida and others; and that the said colonies have flourished under the protection of our august house for ages past; have never been emancipated therefrom; and yet have hitherto yielded little profit to the same; and whereas we ourself have in the last war fought for and defended the said colonies against the power of France, and thereby enabled them to make conquests from the said power in America, for which we have not yet received adequate compensation; and whereas it is just and expedient that a revenue should be raised from the said colonies in Britain towards our indemnification; and that those who are descendants of our ancient subjects, and thence still owe us due obedience, should contribute to the replenishing of our royal coffers (as they must have done, had their ancestors remained in the territories now to us appertaining); we do therefore hereby ordain and command that, from and after the date of these presents, there shall be levied and paid to our officers of the *customs*, on all goods, wares, and merchandises, and on all grain and other produce of the earth, exported from the said Island of Britain, and on all goods of whatever kind imported into the same, a duty of four and a half per cent *ad valorem*, for the use of us and our successors. And that the said duty may more effectually be collected, we do hereby ordain that all ships or vessels bound from Great Britain to any other part of the world, or from any other part of the world to Great Britain, shall in their respective voyages touch at our port of Königsberg, there to be unladen, searched, and charged with the said duties.

"And whereas there hath been from time to time discovered in the said Island of Great Britain, by our colonists there, many mines or beds of iron stone; and sundry subjects of our ancient dominion, skilful in converting the said stone into metal, have in time past transported themselves thither, carrying with them and communicating that art; and the inhabitants of the said Island, presuming that they had a natural right to make the best use they could of the natural productions of their country for their own benefit, have not only built furnaces for smelting the said stone into iron, but have erected plating-forges, slitting-mills, and steel-furnaces for the more convenient manu-facturing of the same; thereby endangering a diminution of the said manufacture in our ancient dominion; – We do therefore hereby farther ordain that, from and after the date hereof, no mill or other engine for slitting or rolling of iron, or any plating-forge to work with a tilt-hammer, or any furnace for making steel, shall be erected or continued in the said Island of Great Britain. And the Lord Lieutenant of every county in the said Island is hereby commanded, on information of any such erection within his county to order, and by force to cause, the same to be abated and destroyed; as he shall answer the neglect thereof to us at his peril. But we are nevertheless graciously pleased to permit the inhabitants of the said Island to transport their iron into Prussia, there to be manufactured, and to them returned; they paying our Prussian subjects for the workmanship, with all the costs of commission, freight, and risk, coming and returning; anything herein contained to the contrary notwithstanding.

"We do not, however, think fit to extend this our in-dulgence to the article of *wool*; but meaning to encourage not only the manufacturing of woolen cloth but also the raising of wool in our ancient dominions, and to prevent both, as much as may be, in our said Island, we do hereby absolutely forbid the transportation of wool from thence, even to the mother country, Prussia; and that those island-ers may be farther and more effectually restrained in mak-ing any advantage of their own wool in the way of manu-facture, we command that none shall be carried out of one county into another; nor shall any worsted, bay, or woolen yarn, cloth, says, bays, kerseys, serges, frizes, druggets, clothserges, shalloons, or any other drapery stuffs or woolen manufactures whatsoever, made up or mixed with wool in any of the said counties, be carried into any other county, or be water-borne even across the smallest river or creek; on penalty of forfeiture of the same, together with the boats, carriages, horses, etc., that shall be employed in removing them. Nevertheless, our loving subjects there are hereby permitted (if they think proper) to use all their wool as manure for the improvement of their lands.

"And whereas the art and mystery of making *hats* hath arrived at great perfection in Prussia, and the making of hats by our remoter subjects ought to be as much as possible restrained; and forasmuch as the islanders before mentioned, being in possession of wool, beaver and other furs, have presumptuously conceived they had a right to make some advantage thereof, by manufacturing the same into hats to the prejudice of our domestic manufacture; we do therefore hereby strictly command and ordain that no hats or felts whatsoever, dyed or undyed, finished or unfinished, shall be loaded or put into or upon any vessel, cart, carriage, or horse, to be transported or conveyed out of one county in the said Island into another county, or to any other place whatsoever, by any person or persons whatsoever; on pain of forfeiting the same, with a penalty of five hundred pounds sterling for every offence. Nor shall any hat-maker in any of the said counties employ more than two apprentices, on penalty of five pounds sterling per month; we intending hereby that such hat-makers, being so restrained both in the production and sale of their commodity, may find no advantage in continuing their business. But, lest the said Islanders should suffer inconveniency by the want of hats, we are farther graciously pleased to permit them to send their beaver furs to Prussia; and we also permit hats made thereof to be exported from Prussia to Britain; the people thus favored to pay all costs and charges of manufacturing, interest, commission to our merchants, insurance and freight going and returning, as in the case of iron.

"And, lastly, being willing farther to favor our said

colonies in Britain, we do hereby also ordain and command that all the *thieves*, highway and street robbers, housebreakers, forgerers, murderers, s-d-tes, and villains of every denomination, who have forfeited their lives to the law in Prussia but whom we, in our great clemency, do not think fit here to hang, shall be emptied out of our jails into the said Island of Great Britain, for the better peopling of that country.

"We flatter ourselves, that these our royal regulations and commands will be thought *just and reasonable* by our much-favored colonists in England; the said regulations being copied from their Statutes of 10th and 11th William III. c. 10, 5th George II. c. 22, 23rd George II. c. 29, 4th George I. c. 11, and from other equitable laws made by their Parliaments; or from instructions given by their princes; or from resolutions of both Houses, entered into for the good government of their *own colonies in Ireland and America.*

"And all persons in the said Island are hereby cautioned not to oppose in any wise the execution of this our Edict, or any part thereof, such opposition being high treason; of which all who are suspected shall be transported in fetters from Britain to Prussia, there to be tried and executed according to the Prussian law.

"Such is our pleasure.

"Given at Potsdam, this twenty-fifth day of the month of August, one thousand seven hundred and seventy-three, and in the thirty-third year of our reign.

"By the King, in his Council.

"RECHTMAESSIG, *Sec.*"

Some take this Edict to be merely one of the King's *jeux d'esprit*;* others suppose it serious, and that he means a quarrel with England; but all here think the assertion it concludes with, "that these regulations are copied from acts of the English Parliament respecting their colonies," a

* jokes

very injurious one, it being impossible to believe that a people distinguished for their love of liberty, a nation so wise, so liberal in its sentiments, so just and equitable towards its neighbors, should, from mean and injudicious views of petty immediate profit, treat its own children in a manner so arbitrary and tyrannical!

INTRODUCING THOMAS PAINE

The publication, in January, 1776, of the pamphlet "Common Sense" helped to crystallize American sentiment for independence. By the spring of that year there was not an adult in the colonies who had not read it or heard its stirring arguments. Its author, Thomas Paine, got his start in America through Franklin, who sent him with a letter of introduction to his son-in-law, Richard Bache, in Philadelphia. In his first letter to Franklin from Philadelphia, in March, 1775, Paine wrote: "Your countenancing me has obtained for me many friends and much reputation, for which please to accept my sincere thanks. I have been applied to by several gentlemen to instruct their sons on very advantageous terms to myself; and a printer and bookseller here, a man of reputation and property, Robert Aitkin, has lately attempted a magazine, but having little or no turn that way himself he has applied to me for assistance. He had not above six hundred subscribers when I first assisted him. We have now upwards of fifteen hundred, and daily increasing. I have not entered into terms with him. This is only the second number. The first I was not concerned in."

London, September 30 1774

Dear Son: The bearer, Mr. Thomas Paine, is very well recommended to me as an ingenious, worthy young man. He goes to Pennsylvania with a view of settling there. I

123

request you to give him your best advice and countenance, as he is quite a stranger there. If you can put him in a way of obtaining employment as a clerk, or assistant tutor in a school, or assistant surveyor (of all which I think him very capable) so that he may procure a subsistence at least till he can make acquaintance and obtain a knowledge of the country, you will do well and much oblige your affectionate father.

THE WAR YEARS
DIPLOMAT AND PHILOSOPHER
IN FRANCE

A week after the American colonies adopted their Declaration of Independence, the British fleet anchored off New York. It was under the command of Lord Howe, Admiral and Member of Parliament, who a year earlier had dealt with Franklin in London in an effort to prevent war between Britain and America. On this occasion Howe was again empowered to try to make peace, and he attempted to deal directly with Franklin, now back in Philadelphia, instead of with Congress. After consulting with Congress, Franklin sent the following reply.

Directing pardons to be offered the colonies, who are the very parties injured, express indeed that opinion of our ignorance, baseness and insensibility which your uninformed and proud nation has long been pleased to entertain of us; but it can have no other effect than that of increasing our resentments. It is impossible we should think of submission to a government that has with the most wanton barbarity and cruelty burnt our defenceless towns in the midst of winter, excited the savages to massacre our farmers and our slaves to murder their masters, and is even now bringing foreign mercenaries to deluge our settlements with blood. These atrocious injuries have extinguished every remaining spark of affection for that parent country we once held so dear; but were it possible for *us* to forget and forgive them, it is not possible for *you* (I mean the British nation) to forgive the people you have so heavily injured. You can never confide again in those as fellow-subjects, and permit them to enjoy equal freedom, to whom you know you have given such just cause of lasting enmity. And this must impel you, were we again under your government, to endeavor the breaking our spirit by the severest tyranny, and obstructing by every means in your power our growing strength and prosperity.

But your Lordship mentions "the King's paternal solicitude for promoting the establishment of lasting *peace* and union with the colonies." If by peace is here meant a peace to be entered into between Britain and America, as distinct states now at war, and his Majesty has given your Lordship powers to treat with us of such a peace, I may venture to say, though without authority, that I think a treaty for that purpose not yet quite impracticable, before we enter into foreign alliances. But I am persuaded you have no such powers. Your nation, though, by punishing those American governors who have created and fomented the discord, rebuilding our burnt towns and repairing as far as possible the mischiefs done us, might yet recover a great share of our regard, and the greatest part of our growing commerce, with all the advantage of that additional strength to be derived from a friendship with us; but I know too well her abounding pride and deficient wisdom to believe she will ever take such salutary measures. Her fondness for conquest, as a warlike nation, her lust of dominion as an ambitious one, and her thirst for a gainful monopoly as a commercial one (none of them legitimate causes of war) will all join to hide from her eyes every view of her true interests and continually goad her on in those ruinous distant expeditions, so destructive both of lives and treasure, that must prove as pernicious to her in the end as the crusades formerly were to most of the nations of Europe.

I have not the vanity, my Lord, to think of intimidating by thus predicting the effects of this war; for I know it will in England have the fate of all my former predictions, not to be believed till the event shall verify it.

Long did I endeavor, with unfeigned and unwearied zeal, to preserve from breaking that fine and noble china vase, the British Empire; for I knew that, being once broken, the separate parts could not retain even their shares of the strength or value that existed in the whole, and that a perfect reunion of those parts could scarce ever be hoped for. Your Lordship may possibly remember the tears of joy that wet my cheek when, at your good sister's in London, you once gave me expectations that a reconciliation might soon take place. I had the misfortune to find those expectations disappointed, and to be treated as the cause of the mischief I was laboring to prevent. My consolation under that groundless and malevolent treatment was that I retained the friendship of many wise and good men in that country, and, among the rest, some share in the regard of Lord Howe.

The well-founded esteem, and, permit me to say, affection which I shall always have for your Lordship, makes it painful to me to see you engaged in conducting a war the great ground of which, as expressed in your letter, is "the necessity of preventing the American trade from passing into foreign channels." To me it seems that neither the obtaining or retaining of any trade, how valuable soever, is an object for which men may justly spill each other's blood; that the true and sure means of extending and securing commerce is the goodness and cheapness of commodities; and that the profit of no trade can ever be equal to the expense of compelling it, and of holding it, by fleets and armies.

I consider this war against us, therefore, as both unjust and unwise; and I am persuaded that cool, dispassionate posterity will condemn to infamy those who advised it; and that even success will not save from some degree of dishonor those who voluntarily engaged to conduct it. I know your great motive in coming hither was the hope of being instrumental in a reconciliation; and I believe, when you find *that* to be impossible on any terms given you to propose, you will relinquish so odious a command and return to a more honorable private station.

– Philadelphia, July 20 1776

America I shall not surrender my liberty and property but with my life. It is not true that my country was planted at your expense. Your own records refute that falsehood to your face. Nor did you ever afford me a man or a shilling to defend me against the Indians, the only enemies I had upon my own account. But when you have quarreled with all Europe, and drawn me with you into all your broils, then you value yourself upon protecting me from the enemies you have made for me. I have no natural cause of difference with Spain, France or Holland, and yet by turns I have joined with you in wars against them all. You would not suffer me to make or keep a separate peace with any of them, though I might easily have done it to great advantage. Does your protecting me in those wars give you a right to fleece me? If so, as I fought for you as well as you for me, it gives me a proportionate right to fleece you.

What think you of an American law to make a monopoly of you and your commerce, as you have done by your laws of me and mine?

Content yourself with that monopoly if you are wise, and learn justice if you would be respected!

Britain You impudent b———h! Am I not your mother country? Is not that a sufficient title to your respect and obedience?

Saxony Mother country! Ha! ha! ha! What respect have *you* the front to claim as a mother country? You know that *I* am *your* mother country, and yet you pay me none. Nay, it is but the other day that you hired ruffians to rob me on the highway and burn my house! For shame! Hide your face and hold your tongue. If you continue this conduct, you will make yourself the contempt of Europe!

Britain O Lord, Where are my friends?

France, Spain, Holland and Saxony, all together Friends! Believe us, you have none, nor ever will have any, till you mend your manners. How can we, who are your neighbors, have any regard for you or expect any equity from you, should your power increase, when we see how basely and unjustly you have used both your *own mother and your own children*?

HOW TO DEAL WITH SPIES

I am much obliged to you for your kind attention to my welfare in the information you give me. I have no doubt of its being well founded. But as it is impossible to discover in every case the falsity of pretended friends who would know our affairs, and more so to prevent being watched by spies when interested people may think proper to place them for that purpose, I have long observed one rule which prevents any inconvenience from such practices. It is simply this: to be concerned in no affairs that I would blush to have made public, and to do nothing but what spies may see and welcome. When a man's actions are just and honorable, the more they are known the more his reputation is increased and established. If I was sure therefore that my *valet de place* was a spy, as probably he is, I think I should not discharge him for that, if in other respects I liked him. The various conjectures you mention concerning my business here must have their course. They amuse those that make them and some of those that hear them; they do me no harm, and therefore it is not necessary that I should take the least pains to rectify them. . . .

– From a letter to Juliana Ritchie
Paris, January 19 1777

MODEL LETTER OF RECOMMENDATION

As American commissioner in France, Franklin was plagued with requests for letters of recommendation for French officers seeking posts in the American Army.

He wrote a friend: "You can have no conception how I am harassed. All my friends are sought out and teased to tease me. Great officers of all ranks, in all departments; ladies, great and small, besides professed solicitors, worry me from morning till night. I am afraid to accept an invitation to dine abroad, being almost sure of meeting with some officer or officer's friend who, as soon as I am put in good humor by a glass or two of champagne, begins his attack on me."

In his vexation he wrote a "Model Letter of Recommendation" which his grandson claimed that he actually used to shame some insistent applicants.

Paris, April 2 1777

Sir: The bearer of this, who is going to America, presses me to give him a letter of recommendation, though I know nothing of him, not even his name. This may seem extraordinary, but I assure you it is not uncommon here. Sometimes, indeed, one unknown person brings another equally unknown, to recommend him; and sometimes they recommend one another! As to this gentleman, I must refer you to himself for his character and merits, with which he is certainly better acquainted than I can possibly be. I recommend him, however, to those civilities which every stranger of whom one knows no harm has a right to; and I request you will do him all the good offices and show him all the favor that, on further acquaintance, you shall find him to deserve.

THE CAUSE OF ALL MANKIND

All Europe is on our side of the question, as far as applause and good wishes can carry them. Those who live under arbitrary power do nevertheless approve of liberty and wish for it; they almost despair of recovering it in Europe; they read the translations of our separate colony constitutions with rapture; and there are such numbers everywhere who talk of removing to America with their families and fortunes, as soon as peace and our independence shall be established, that it is generally believed we shall have a prodigious addition of strength, wealth and arts from the emigrations of Europe; and it is thought that, to lessen or prevent such emigrations, the tyrannies established there must relax, and allow more liberty to their people. Hence it is a common observation here that our cause is *the cause of all mankind,* and that we are fighting for their liberty in defending our own. It is a glorious task assigned us by Providence; which has, I trust, given us spirit and virtue equal to it, and will at last crown it with success. . . .

– From a letter to Samuel Cooper
Paris, May 1 1777

FOR A TORY LADY

You are too early, *hussy,* as well as too saucy, in calling me *rebel;* you should wait for the event, which will determine whether it is a *rebellion* or only a *revolution.* Here the ladies are more civil; they call us *les insurgés,* a character that usually pleased them; and methinks all other women who smart, or have smarted, under the tyranny of a bad husband, ought to be fixed in *revolution* principles, and act accordingly.

On my way to Canada last spring I saw dear Mrs. Barrow at New York. Mr. Barrow had been from her two or three months, to keep Governor Tryon and other Tories company on board the *Asia,* one of the King's ships which lay in the harbor; and in all that time that naughty man had not ventured once on shore to see her. Our troops were then pouring into the town, and she was packing up

134

to leave it, fearing, as she had a large house, they would incommode her by quartering officers in it. As she appeared in great perplexity, scarce knowing where to go, I persuaded her to stay; and I went to the general officers then commanding there and recommended her to their protection; which they promised and performed. On my return from Canada, where I was a piece of a governor (and I think a very good one) for a fortnight, and might have been so till this time if your wicked army, enemies to all good government, had not come and driven me out, I found her still in quiet possession of her house. I inquired how our people had behaved to her. She spoke in high terms of the respectful attention they had paid her, and the quiet and security they had procured her. I said I was glad of it; and that, if they had used her ill, I would have become Tory.

"Then," said she, with that pleasing gaiety so natural to her, "*I wish they had.*"

For you must know she is a *Toryess* as well as you, and can as flippantly call *rebel*. I drank tea with her; we talked affectionately of you and our other friends the Wilkses, of whom she had received no late intelligence. What became of her since, I have not heard. The street she lived in was some months after chiefly burnt down; but as the town was then, and ever since has been, in possession of the King's troops, I have had no opportunity of knowing if she suffered any loss in the conflagration. I hope she did not, as, if she did, I should wish I had not persuaded her to stay there. . . .

Pray learn, if you have not already learned, like me, to be pleased with other people's pleasures, and happy with their happiness, when none occur to your own; and then perhaps you will not so soon be weary of the place you chance to be in, and so fond of rambling to get rid of your *ennui*. I fancy you have hit upon the right reason of your being weary of St. Omer's, *viz.,* that you are out of temper, which is the effect of full living and idleness. A month in

Bridewell, beating hemp, upon bread and water, would give you health and spirits, and subsequent cheerfulness and contentment with every other situation. I prescribe that regimen for you, my dear, in pure good-will, without a fee. And let me tell you, if you do not get into temper neither Brussels nor Lisle will suit you. I know nothing of the price of living in either of those places; but I am sure a single woman, as you are, might with economy upon two hundred pounds a year maintain herself comfortably anywhere, and me into the bargain. Do not invite me in earnest, however, to come and live with you; for, being posted here, I ought not to comply, and I am not sure I should be able to refuse.

Present my respects to Mrs. Payne and Mrs. Heathcot; for though I have not the honor of knowing them, yet as you say they are friends to the American cause I am sure they must be women of good understanding. I know you wish you could see me; but as you cannot, I will describe myself to you. Figure me in your mind as jolly as formerly, and as strong and hearty, only a few years older; very plainly dressed, wearing my thin, grey straight hair that peeps out under my only *coiffure*, a fine fur cap, which comes down my forehead almost to my spectacles. Think how this must appear among the powdered heads of Paris! I wish every lady and gentleman in France would only be so obliging as to follow my fashion, comb their own heads as I do mine, dismiss their *friseurs*, and pay me half the money they paid to them. You see, the gentry might well afford this, and I could then enlist these *friseurs*, who are at least a hundred thousand, and with the money I would maintain them, make a visit with them to England, and dress the heads of your ministers and privy councillors; which I conceive at present to be *un peu dérangées**. Adieu, madcap; and believe me ever your affectionate friend and humble servant. . . .

* A little disturbed

P. S. Don't be proud of this long letter. A fit of the gout, which has confined me five days and made me refuse to receive company, has given me a little time to trifle; otherwise it would have been very short, visitors and business would have interrupted; and perhaps, with Mrs. Barrow, you wish they had.

> – Letter to Mrs. Emma Thompson
> Paris, February 8 1777

A FAMOUS FATHER TO HIS DAUGHTER

Passy, June 3 1779

Dear Sally*: I have before me your letters of October 22nd and January 17th. They are the only ones I received from you in the course of eighteen months. If you knew how happy your letters make me, and considered how many miscarry, I think you would write oftener. . . .

The clay medallion of me you say you gave to Mr. Hopkinson was the first of the kind made in France. A variety of others have been made since of different sizes; some to be set in the lids of snuffboxes and some are so small as to be worn in rings; and the numbers sold are incredible. These, with the pictures, busts and prints (of which copies upon copies are spread everywhere) have made your father's face as well known as that of the moon, so that he durst not do anything that would oblige him to run away, as his phiz would discover him wherever he should venture to show it. It is said by learned etymologists that the name *doll*, for the images children play with, is derived from the word IDOL. From the number of *dolls* now made of him, he may truly be said, *in that sense,* to be *i-doll-ized* in this country. . . .

I was charmed with the account you gave me of your industry, the tablecloths of your own spinning, etc.; but the

* Mrs. Sarah Bache, in Philadelphia

latter part of the paragraph, that you had sent for linen from France because weaving and flax were grown dear, alas, that dissolved the charm; and your sending for long black pins, and lace and *feathers*! disgusted me as much as if you had put salt into my strawberries. The spinning, I see, is laid aside, and you are to be dressed for the ball! You seem not to know, my dear daughter, that of all the dear things in this world, idleness is dearest, except mischief. . . .

When I began to read your account of the high prices of goods, "a pair of gloves seven dollars, a yard of common gauze twenty-four dollars, and that it now required a fortune to maintain a family in a very plain way," I expected you would conclude with telling me that everyone as well as yourself was grown frugal and industrious; and I could scarce believe my eyes in reading forward that "there never was so much pleasure and dressing going on"; and that you yourself wanted black pins and feathers from France, to appear, I suppose, in the mode! This leads me to imagine that perhaps it is not so much that the goods are grown dear as that the money is grown cheap, as everything else will do when excessively plenty; and that people are still as easy nearly in their circumstances as when a pair of gloves might be had for half a crown. The war indeed might in some degree raise the prices of goods, and the high taxes which are necessary to support the war may make our frugality necessary; and as I am always preaching that doctrine I cannot, in conscience or in decency, encourage the contrary by my example in furnishing my children with foolish modes and luxuries. I therefore send all the articles you desire that are useful and necessary and omit the rest; for, as you say you should "have great pride in wearing anything I send, and showing it as your father's taste," I must avoid giving you an opportunity of doing that with either lace or feathers. If you wear your cambric ruffles as I do, and take care not to mend the holes, they will come in time to be lace; and feathers, my dear girl, may be had in America from every cock's tail.

If you happen again to see General Washington, assure him of my very great and sincere respects, and tell him that all the old Generals here amuse themselves in studying the accounts of his operations, and approve highly of his conduct.

Present my affectionate regards to all friends that inquire after me . . . and write oftener, my dear child, to your loving father.

TO GEORGE WASHINGTON

Passy, March 16 1780

Sir: I have received but lately the letter your Excellency* did me the honor of writing to me in recommendation of the Marquis de Lafayette**. His modesty detained it long in his own hands. We became acquainted, however, from the time of his arrival at Paris; and his zeal for the honor of our country, his activity in our affairs here, and his firm attachment to our cause and to you, impressed me with the same regard and esteem for him that your Excellency's letter would have done, had it been immediately delivered to me.

* George Washington (1732–1799) was commander-in-chief of the American armies in the Revolutionary War and was elected first president of the United States in 1789. He and Franklin held each other in high esteem. In his will Franklin left to Washington "my fine crab-tree stick, with a gold head curiously wrought in the form of the cap of liberty . . . to my friend and the friend of mankind . . . If it were a sceptre, he has merited it and would become it."

** The Marquis de Lafayette (1757–1834), a reserve officer in the French army, joined Washington's forces at the age of nineteen, became a major general, and was presented with a sword by Congress in acknowledgment of his bravery.

Should peace arrive after another campaign or two, and afford us a little leisure, I should be happy to see your Excellency in Europe and to accompany you, if my age and strength would permit, in visiting some of its ancient and most famous kingdoms. You would, on this side of the sea, enjoy the great reputation you have acquired, pure and free from those little shades that the jealousy and envy of a man's countrymen and contemporaries are ever endeavoring to cast over living merit. Here you would know, and enjoy, what posterity will say of Washington. For a thousand leagues have nearly the same effect with a thousand years. The feeble voice of those groveling passions cannot extend so far either in time or distance. At present I enjoy that pleasure for you; as I frequently hear the old generals of this martial country, who study the maps of America, and mark upon them all your operations, speak with sincere approbation and great applause of your conduct, and join in giving you the character of one of the greatest captains of the age.

I must soon quit this scene, but you may live to see our country flourish, as it will amazingly and rapidly after the war is over: like a field of young Indian corn, which long fair weather and sunshine had enfeebled and discolored, and which, in that weak state, by a thunder-gust of violent wind, hail, and rain seemed to be threatened with absolute destruction; yet the storm being past, it recovers fresh verdure, shoots up with double vigor, and delights the eye, not of its owner only but of every observing traveler.

ON DIPLOMATIC ETIQUETTE

It seems to me that we have, in most instances, hurt our credit and importance by sending all over Europe, begging alliances, and soliciting declarations of our independence. The nations, perhaps from thence, seemed to think that our independence is something they have to sell, and that we do not offer enough for it. Mr. Adams has succeeded in Holland, owing to their war with England and a good deal to the late votes in the Commons towards a reconciliation; but the ministers of the other powers refused, as I hear, to return his visits, because our independence was not yet acknowledged by their courts. I had heard here, by good luck, that the same resolution was taken by several of them not to return the visits I should make them (as they supposed) when I was first received here as minister plenipotentiary, and disappointed their project by visiting none of them. In my private opinion, the first civility is due from the old resident to the stranger and newcomer. My opinion indeed is good for nothing against custom, which I should have obeyed, but for the circumstances that rendered it more prudent to avoid disputes and affronts, though at the hazard of being thought rude or singular.

While I am writing, something ridiculous enough on this head has happened to me. The Count du Nord, who is son of the Empress of Russia, arriving at Paris ordered, it seems, cards of visit to be sent to all the foreign ministers. One of them, on which was written, *Le Comte du Nord et le Prince Bariatinski*, was brought to me. It was on Monday evening last. Being at court the next day, I inquired of an old minister, my friend, what was the etiquette, and whether the Count received visits. The answer was, *Non, on se fait écrire; voilà tout**. This is done by passing the door and ordering your name to be written on the porter's book. Accordingly, on Wednesday I passed the house of Prince Bariatinski, ambassador of Russia, where the Count lodged, and left my name on the list of each. I thought no more of the matter; but this day, May the 24th, comes the servant who brought the card in great affliction, saying he was like to be ruined by his mistake in bringing the card here, and wishing to obtain from me some paper, of I know not what kind, for I did not see him.

* "No, one has oneself written down; that is all."

In the afternoon came my friend, M. Le Roy, who is also a friend of the Prince's, telling me how much he, the Prince, was concerned at the accident, that both himself and the Count had great personal regard for me and my character, but that our independence not yet being acknowledged by the court of Russia, it was impossible for him to permit himself to make me a visit as minister. I told M. Le Roy it was not my custom to seek such honors, though I was very sensible of them when conferred upon me; that I should not have voluntarily intruded a visit, and that, in this case, I had only done what I was informed the etiquette required of me; but if it would be attended with any inconvenience to Prince Bariatinski, whom I much esteemed and respected, I thought the remedy was easy; he had only to erase my name out of his book of visits received, and I would burn their card.

All the northern princes are not ashamed of a little civility committed towards an American. The King of Denmark, traveling in England under an assumed name, sent me a card, expressing in strong terms his esteem for me and inviting me to dinner with him at St. James's. And the ambassador from the King of Sweden lately asked me whether I had powers to make a treaty of commerce with their kingdom for, he said, his master was desirous of such a treaty with the United States, and directed him to ask me the question, and had charged him to tell me that it would flatter him greatly to make it with a person whose character he so much esteemed, etc. Such compliments might make me a little proud, if we Americans were not naturally as much so already as the porter, who, being told he had with his burden jostled the Great Czar Peter, then in London, walking the street;

"Poh!" says he, "we are all Czars here." ...

> – From the *Journal of the Negotiation
> For Peace With Great Britain*
> 1781–82

BLESSED ARE THE PEACEMAKERS

To John Adams

Passy, October 12 1781

Sir: I received the letter your Excellency did me the honor of writing to me the 4th instant. I have never known a peace made, even the most advantageous, that was not censured as inadequate, and the makers condemned as injudicious or corrupt. *Blessed are the peacemakers* is, I suppose, to be understood in the other world; for in this they are frequently *cursed.* Being as yet rather too much attached to this world, I had therefore no ambition to be concerned in fabricating this peace, and know not how I came to be put into the commission*. I esteem it, however, as an honor to be joined with you in so important a business; and if the execution of it shall happen in my time, which I hardly expect, I shall endeavor to assist in discharging the duty according to the best of my judgment. . . .

A FABLE

Written after the Revolution, referring to the claims of the American Loyalists on the British Government.

Lion, king of a certain forest, had among his subjects a body of faithful dogs, in principle and affection strongly attached to his person and government, and through whose

* Actually Franklin played a major role in fabricating the peace with Great Britain. He was appointed to a five-member commission but he conducted the preliminary negotiations alone, joined several months later by John Adams and John Jay. The final treaty was signed in Paris on September 3 1783. John Adams became the first vice-president and the second president of the United States.

assistance he had extended his dominions and had become the terror of his enemies.

Lion, however, influenced by evil counselors, took an aversion to the dogs, condemned them unheard, and ordered his tigers, leopards, and panthers to attack and destroy them.

The dogs petitioned humbly but their petitions were rejected haughtily; and they were forced to defend themselves, which they did with bravery.

A few among them, of a mongrel race, derived from a mixture with wolves and foxes, corrupted by royal promises of great rewards, deserted the honest dogs and joined their enemies.

The dogs were finally victorious; a treaty of peace was made in which Lion acknowledged them to be free, and disclaimed all future authority over them.

The mongrels, not being permitted to return among them, claimed of the royalists the reward that had been promised.

A council of the beasts was held to consider their demand.

The wolves and the foxes agreed unanimously that the demand was just, that royal promises ought to be kept, and that every loyal subject should contribute freely to enable his Majesty to fulfill them.

The horse alone, with a boldness and freedom that became the nobleness of his nature, delivered a contrary opinion.

"The King," said he, "has been misled by bad ministers to war unjustly upon his faithful subjects. Royal promises, when made to encourage us to act for the public good, should indeed be honorably acquitted; but if to encourage us to betray and destroy each other, they are wicked and void from the beginning. The advisers of such promises, and those who murdered in consequence of them, instead of being recompensed, should be severely punished. Consider how greatly our common strength is already diminished by our loss of the dogs. If you enable the King to reward those fratricides, you will establish a precedent that may justify a future tyrant in making like promises; and every example of such an unnatural brute rewarded will give them additional weight. Horses and bulls, as well as dogs, may thus be divided against their own kind, and civil wars produced at pleasure, till we are so weakened that neither liberty nor safety is any longer to be found in the forest, and nothing remains but abject submission to the will of a despot, who may devour us as he pleases."

The council had sense enough to resolve – that the demand be rejected.

HEREDITARY HONORS

News had reached Franklin of the formation of the Society of Cincinnati, with George Washington at its head.

I only wonder that, when the united wisdom of our nation had, in the articles of confederation, manifested their dislike of establishing ranks of nobility, by authority either of the Congress or of any particular State, a number of private persons should think proper to distinguish themselves and their posterity from their fellow citizens, and form an order of *hereditary knights,* in direct opposition to the solemnly declared sense of their country! . . . .

Honor, worthily obtained (as that for example of our officers) is in its nature a *personal* thing, and incommunicable to any but those who had some share in obtaining it. Thus among the Chinese the most ancient and from long experience the wisest of nations, honor does not *descend* but *ascends.* If a man from his learning, his wisdom, or his valor, is promoted by the Emperor to the rank of Mandarin, his parents are immediately entitled to all the same ceremonies of respect from the people that are established as due to the Mandarin himself, on the supposition that it must have been owing to the education, instruction and good example afforded him by his parents that he was rendered capable of serving the public. . . .

I wish, therefore, that the Cincinnati, if they must go on with their project, would direct the badges of their order to be worn by their fathers and mothers, instead of handing them down to their children. It would be a good precedent, and might have good effects. It would also be a kind of obedience to the fourth commandment, in which God enjoins us to *honor* our father and mother, but has nowhere directed us to honor our children. And certainly no mode of honoring those immediate authors of our being can be more effectual than that of doing praiseworthy actions which reflect honor on those who gave us our education, or more becoming than that of manifesting, by some public expression or token, that it is to their instruction and example we ascribe the merit of those actions.

But the absurdity of *descending honors* is not a mere matter of philosophical opinion; it is capable of mathematical demonstration. A man's son, for instance, is but half his family, the other half belonging to the family of his wife. His son too, marrying into another family, his share in the grandson is but a fourth; in the great grandson, by the same process, it is but an eighth; in the next generation a sixteenth; the next a thirty-second; the next a sixty-fourth; the next an hundred and twenty-eighth; the next a two hundred and fifty-sixth; and the next a five hundred and twelfth; thus in nine generations, which will not require more than three hundred years (no very great antiquity for a family), our present Chevalier of the Order of Cincinnatus's share in the then existing knight will be but a five hundred and twelfth part; which, allowing the present certain fidelity of American wives to be insured down through all those nine generations, is so small a consideration that methinks no reasonable man would hazard for the sake of it the disagreeable consequences of the jealousy, envy, and ill-will of his countrymen.

Let us go back with our calculation from this young noble, the five hundred and twelfth part of the present knight, through his nine generations, till we return to the year of institution. He must have had a father and mother, they are two; each of them had a father and mother, they are four. Those of the next preceding generation will be eight, the next sixteen, the next thirty-two, the next sixty-four, the next one hundred and twenty-eight, the next two hundred and fifty-six, and the ninth in this retrocession five hundred and twelve, who must be now existing and all contribute their proportion to this future Chevalier de Cincinnatus. These, with the rest, make together as follows:

$$
\begin{array}{r}
2 \\
4 \\
8 \\
16 \\
32 \\
64 \\
128 \\
256 \\
512 \\
\hline
\text{Total} \quad 1022 \\
\end{array}
$$

One thousand and twenty-two men and women, contributors to the formation of one knight. And if we are to have a thousand of these future knights, there must be now and hereafter existing one million and twenty-two thousand fathers and mothers who are to contribute to their production, unless a part of the number are employed in making more knights than one. Let us strike off, then, the twenty-two thousand on the supposition of this double employ, and then consider whether, after a reasonable estimation of the number of rogues and fools and scoundrels and prostitutes that are mixed with and necessarily help to make up their millions of predecessors, posterity will have much reason to boast of the noble blood of the then existing set of Chevaliers of Cincinnatus. The future genealogists, too, of these Chevaliers, in proving the lineal descent of their honor through so many generations (even supposing honor capable in its nature of descending), will discover only the small share of this honor which can be justly claimed by any one of them, since the above simple process in arithmetic makes it quite plain and clear that, in proportion as the antiquity of the family shall augment, the right to the honor of the ancestor will diminish, and a few generations more would reduce it to something so small as to be near an absolute nullity. I hope, therefore, that the Order will drop this part of their project, and content themselves, as the Knights of the Garter, Bath, Thistle, St. Louis, and other Orders of Europe do, with a life enjoyment of their little badge and riband, and let the distinction die with those who have merited it. This I imagine will give no offence. For my own part, I shall think it a convenience when I go into a company where there may be faces unknown to me if I discover, by this badge, the persons who merit some particular expression of my respect; and it will save modest virtue the trouble of calling for our regard by awkward roundabout intimations of having been heretofore employed as officers in the Continental service. . . .

> – From a letter to Mrs. Sarah Bache,
> Franklin's daughter
> Passy, January 26 1784

REMARKS
CONCERNING THE SAVAGES
OF NORTH AMERICA

Savages we call them because their manners differ from ours, which we think the perfection of civility; they think the same of theirs.

Perhaps if we could examine the manners of different nations with impartiality we should find no people so rude as to be without any rules of politeness; nor any so polite as not to have some remains of rudeness.

The Indian men, when young, are hunters and warriors; when old, counselors; for all their government is by the counsel or advice of the sages; there is no force, there are no prisons, no officers to compel obedience, or inflict punishment. Hence they generally study oratory, the best speaker having the most influence. The Indian women till the ground, dress the food, nurse and bring up the children, and preserve and hand down to posterity the memory of public transactions. These employments of men and women are accounted natural and honorable. Having few artificial wants, they have abundance of leisure for improvement by conversation. Our laborious manner of life, compared with theirs, they esteem slavish and base, and the learning on which we value ourselves they regard as frivolous and useless. An instance of this occurred at the treaty of Lancaster in Pennsylvania, *anno* 1744, between the government of Virginia and the Six Nations. After the principal business was settled, the commissioners from Virginia acquainted the Indians by a speech that there was at Williamsburg a college with a fund for educating Indian youth, and that if the chiefs of the Six Nations would send down half a dozen of their sons to that college the government would take care that they should be well provided for and instructed in all the learning of the white people. It is one of the Indian rules of politeness not to answer a public proposition the same day it is made; they think it would be treating it as a light matter, and that they show it respect by taking time to consider it, as of a matter important. They therefore deferred their answer till the day following, when their speaker began by expressing their deep sense of the kindness of the Virginia government in making them that offer, "for we know," says he, "that you highly esteem the kind of learning taught in those colleges, and that the maintenance of our young men, while with you, would be very expensive to you. We are convinced, therefore, that you mean to do us good by your proposal, and we thank you heartily. But you who are wise must know that different nations have different conceptions of things, and you will therefore not take it amiss if our ideas of this kind of education happen not to be the same as yours. We have had some experience of it; several of our young people were formerly brought up at the colleges of the northern provinces; they were instructed in all your sciences, but when they came back to us they were bad runners, ignorant of every means of living in the woods, unable to bear either cold or hunger, knew neither how to build a cabin, take a deer, nor kill an enemy, spoke our language imperfectly, were therefore neither fit for hunters, warriors nor counselors; they were totally good for nothing. We are, however, not the less obliged by your kind offer, though we decline accepting it, and to show our grateful sense of it, if the gentlemen of Virginia will send us a dozen of their sons, we will take great care of their education, instruct them in all we know, and make *men* of them."

Having frequent occasions to hold public councils, they have acquired great order and decency in conducting them. The old men sit in the foremost ranks, the warriors in the next, and women and children in the hindmost. The business of the women is to take exact notice of what passes, imprint it in their memories (for they have no writing), and communicate it to their children. They are the records of the council, and they preserve the tradition of the stipulations in treating a hundred years back; which, when we compare with our writings we always find exact. He that would speak rises. The rest observe a profound silence. When he has finished and sits down they leave him five or six minutes to recollect, that if he has omitted anything he intended to add he may rise again and deliver it. To interrupt another, even in common conversation, is reckoned highly indecent. How different this is from the conduct of a polite British House of Commons, where scarce a day passes without the confusion that makes the speaker hoarse in calling *to order*; and how different from the mode of conversation in many polite companies of Europe where, if you do not deliver your sentence with great rapidity you are cut off in the middle of it by the impatient loquacity of those you converse with, and never suffered to finish it!

The politeness of these savages in conversation is indeed carried to excess, since it does not permit them to contradict or deny the truth of what is asserted in their presence. By this means they indeed avoid disputes, but then it becomes difficult to know their minds or what impression you have made on them. The missionaries who have attempted to convert them to Christianity all complain of this as one of the great difficulties of their mission. The Indians hear with patience the truths of Gospel explained to them and give their usual tokens of assent and approbation; you would think they were convinced. No such matter. It is mere civility.

A Swedish minister, having assembled the chiefs of the Susquehanna Indians, made a sermon to them, acquainting them with the principal historical facts on which our religion is founded, such as the fall of our first parents by eating the apple, the coming of Christ to repair the mischief, his miracles and suffering, etc. When he had finished, an Indian orator stood up to thank him.

"What you have told us," says he, "is all very good. It is indeed bad to eat apples. It is much better to make them all into cider. We are much obliged by your kindness in coming so far to tell us those things which you have heard from your mothers. In return, I will tell you some of those we have heard from ours.

"In the beginning, our fathers had only the flesh of the animals to subsist on, and if their hunting was unsuccessful, they were starving. Two of our young hunters, having killed a deer, made a fire in the woods to broil some parts of it. When they were about to satisfy their hunger, they beheld a beautiful young woman descend from the clouds and seat herself on that hill which you see yonder among the Blue Mountains. They said to each other, it is a spirit that perhaps has smelled our broiling venison and wishes to eat of it; let us offer some to her. They presented her with the tongue; she was pleased with the taste of it, and said: 'Your kindness shall be rewarded; come to this place after thirteen moons, and you shall find something that will be of great benefit in nourishing you and your children to the latest generations.' They did so, and to their surprise found plants they had never seen before, but which from that ancient time have been constantly cultivated among us, to our great advantage. Where her right hand had touched the ground they found maize; where her left hand had touched it they found kidney beans; where her backside had sat on it they found tobacco."

The good missionary, disgusted with this idle tale, said, "What I delivered to you were sacred truths, but what you tell me is mere fable, fiction and falsehood."

The Indian, offended, replied, "My brother, it seems your friends have not done you justice in your education; they have not well instructed you in the rules of common civility. You saw that we, who understand and practice those rules, believed all your stories; why do you refuse to believe ours? . . . .

– First published as a pamphlet
London, 1784

ON THE CRIMINAL LAWS

These observations blaming the cruel criminal laws of the time on the desire of the wealthy to protect their property were prompted by a treatise by Dr. Madan, an English-man, entitled "Thoughts on Executive Justice," justify-

ing the hanging of thieves. They were written by Franklin in the form of a letter to his friend, Benjamin Vaughan, dated at Passy, March 14 1785. The essay, part of which is reproduced here, was published anonymously in London the following year under the title "A Letter from a Gentleman abroad to his Friend in England" in a small volume by Sir Samuel Romilly, the reformer of English criminal law. Romilly referred to it as "the production of one of the best and most eminent men of the present age."

If we really believe, as we profess to believe, that the law of Moses was the law of God, the dictate of divine wisdom, infinitely superior to human; on what principles do we ordain death as the punishment of an offence which, according to that law, was only to be punished by a restitution of fourfold? To put a man to death for an offence which does not deserve death, is it not a murder? And, as the French writer says, *Doit-on punir un délit contre la société par un crime contre la nature?**

Superfluous property is the creature of society. Simple and mild laws were sufficient to guard the property that was merely necessary. The savage's bow, his hatchet, and his coat of skins were sufficiently secured, without law, by the fear of personal resentment and retaliation. When, by virtue of the first laws, part of the society accumulated wealth and grew powerful, they enacted others more severe, and would protect their property at the expense of humanity. This was abusing their power, and commencing a tyranny. If a savage, before he entered into society, had been told, "Your neighbor by this means may become owner of a hundred deer; but if your brother or your son or yourself, having no deer of your own and being hungry, should kill one, an infamous death must be the consequence"; he would probably have preferred his liberty and his common

* Ought an offence against society to be punished by a crime against nature?

153

right of killing any deer to all the advantages of society that might be proposed to him.

That it is better a hundred guilty persons should escape than that one innocent person should suffer, is a maxim that has been long and generally approved; never, that I know of, controverted. . . .

I see in the last newspapers from London that a woman is capitally convicted at the Old Bailey, for privately stealing out of a shop some gauze, value fourteen shillings and threepence; is there any proportion between the injury done by a theft, value fourteen shillings and threepence, and the punishment of a human creature by death, on a gibbet? Might not the woman, by her labor, have made the reparation ordained by God, in paying fourfold? Is not all punishment inflicted beyond the merit of the offence so much punishment of innocence? In this light, how vast is the annual quantity of not only *injured*, but *suffering* innocence in almost all the civilized states of Europe?

But it seems to have been thought that this kind of innocence may be punished by way of *preventing* crimes. I have read, indeed, of a cruel Turk in Barbary who, whenever he bought a new Christian slave, ordered him immediately to be hung up by the legs and to receive a hundred blows of a cudgel on the soles of his feet, that the severe sense of the punishment, and fear of incurring it thereafter, might prevent the faults that should merit it. Our author himself would hardly approve entirely of this Turk's conduct in the government of slaves; and yet he appears to recommend something like it for the government of English subjects when he applauds the reply of Judge Burnet to the convict horse-stealer who, being asked what he had to say why judgment of death should not pass against him, and answering that it was hard to hang a man for *only* stealing a horse, was told by the judge, "Man, thou art not to be hanged *only* for stealing, but that horses may not be stolen."

The man's answer, if candidly examined, will I imagine

appear reasonable, as founded on the eternal principle of justice and equity that punishments should be proportioned to offences; and the judge's reply brutal and unreasonable, though the writer "wishes all judges to carry it with them whenever they go the circuit, and to bear it in their minds as containing a wise reason for all the penal statutes which they are called upon to put in execution. It at once illustrates," says he, "the true grounds and reasons of all capital punishments whatsoever, namely, that every man's property, as well as his life, may be held sacred and inviolate." Is there then no difference in value between property and life? If I think it right that the crime of murder should be punished with death, not only as an equal punishment of the crime, but to prevent other murders, does it follow that I must approve of inflicting the same punishment for a little invasion on my property by theft? If I am not myself so barbarous, so bloody-minded and revengeful, as to kill a fellow-creature for stealing from me fourteen shillings and threepence, how can I approve of a law, that does it?....

It is said by those who know Europe generally, that there are more thefts committed and punished annually in England than in all the other nations put together. If this be so, there must be a cause or causes for such depravity in your common people. May not one be the deficiency of justice and morality in your national government, manifested in your oppressive conduct to your subjects, and unjust wars on your neighbors? View the long-persisted in, unjust monopolizing treatment of Ireland at length acknowledged? View the plundering government exercised by your merchants in the Indies; the confiscating war made upon the American colonies; and, to say nothing of those upon France and Spain, view the late war upon Holland, which was seen by impartial Europe in no other light than that of a war of rapine and pillage; the hopes of an immense and easy prey being its only apparent, and probably its true and real motive and encouragements.

Justice is as strictly due between neighbor nations as between neighbor citizens. A highwayman is as much a robber when he plunders in a gang as when single; and a nation that makes an unjust war is only a *great gang*. . . .

REFLECTIONS ON WAGES

If the term *wages* be taken in its widest signification, it will be found that almost all the citizens of a large state receive and pay wages. I shall confine my remarks, however, to one description of wages, the only one with which government should intermeddle or which requires its care. I mean the wages of the lowest class, those men without property, without capital, who live solely by the labor of their hands. This is always the most numerous class in a state; and, consequently, that community cannot be pronounced happy in which, from the lowness and insufficiency of wages, the laboring class procure so scanty a subsistence that, barely able to provide for their own necessities, they have not the means of marrying and rearing a family, and are reduced to beggary whenever employment fails them, or age and sickness oblige them to give up work.

Further, the wages under consideration ought not to be estimated by their amount in money, but by the quantity of provisions, clothing, and other commodities which the laborer can procure for the money which he receives.

Unhappily, in all the political states of the old world a numerous class of citizens have nothing to live upon but their wages, and these are inadequate to their support. This is the real cause of the misery of so many day-laborers, who work in the fields or in manufactories in towns; of pauperism, an evil which is spreading every day, more and more, because governments attempt to check it by feeble remedies only; of depravity of morals; and of almost every crime. The policy of tyranny and of commerce has overlooked and disguised these truths. The horrible maxim that the people must be poor in order that they may remain in subjection is still held by many persons of hard hearts and perverted understanding, with whom it were useless to contend. Others, again, think that the people should be poor from a regard for the supposed interests of commerce. They believe that to increase the rate of wages would raise the price of the productions of the soil, and especially of industry, which are sold to foreign nations, and thus that exportation and the profits arising from it would be diminished. But this motive is at once cruel and ill-founded.

It is cruel; for whatever may be the advantages of foreign commerce, if in order to possess them half the nation must languish in misery, we cannot without crime endeavor to obtain them, and it becomes the duty of a government to relinquish them. To desire to keep down the rate of wages with the view of favoring the exportation of merchandise is to seek to render the citizens of a state miserable in order that foreigners may purchase its productions at a cheaper rate; it is, at most attempting to enrich a few merchants by impoverishing the body of the nation; it is taking the part of the stronger in that contest, already so unequal, between the man who can pay wages and him who is under the necessity of receiving them; it is, in one word, to forget that the object of every political society ought to be the happiness of the largest number.

This motive is, moreover, ill-founded; for in order to secure to a nation a profitable export for the products of its agriculture and manufactures it is not necessary that the rate of wages should be reduced so extremely low as we find it in almost all the countries of Europe. It is not the wages of the workman, but the price of the merchandise that should be lowered in order that this merchandise may be sold to foreign nations. But men have always neglected to make this distinction. The wages of the laborer are the price of his day's work. The price of merchandise is the sum it costs to gather the produce of the soil or prepare any product of industry. The price of this production may be very moderate while the laborer may receive good wages, that is, the means of procuring a comfortable subsistence.

The labor necessary to gather or prepare the article to be sold may be cheap, and the wages of the workman good. Although the workmen of Manchester and Norwich and those of Amiens and Abbeville are employed in the same kind of labor, the former receive considerably higher wages than the latter; and yet the woolen fabrics of Manchester and Norwich of the same quality are not so dear as those of Amiens and Abbeville.

It would occupy too much time fully to develop this principle. I will only observe here, that it results in a great measure from the fact that the price of labor in the arts, and even in agriculture, is wonderfully diminished by the perfection of the machinery employed in them, by the intelligence and activity of the workmen, and by the judicious division of labor. Now these methods of reducing the price of manufactured articles have nothing to do with the low wages of the workman. In a large manufactory, where animals are employed instead of men and machinery instead of animal power, and where that judicious division of labor is made which doubles, nay, increases tenfold both power and time, the article can be manufactured and sold at a much lower rate than in those establishments which do not enjoy the same advantages; and yet the workmen in the former may receive twice as much as in the latter. . . .

High wages attract the most skilful and most industrious workmen. Thus the article is better made; it sells better; and in this way, the employer makes a greater profit than he could do by diminishing the pay of the workmen. A good workman spoils fewer tools, wastes less material and works faster than one of inferior skill; and thus the profits of the manufacturer are increased still more.

The perfection of machinery in all the arts is owing in a great degree to the workmen. There is no important manufacture in which they have not invented some useful process which saves time and materials or improves the workmanship. If common articles of manufacture, the only ones worthy to interest the statesman, if woolen, cotton, and even silk stuffs, articles made of iron, steel, copper, skins, leather, and various other things, are generally of better quality, at the same price, in England than in other countries, it is because workmen are there better paid.

The low rate of wages, then, is not the real cause of the advantages of commerce between one nation and another; but it is one of the greatest evils of political communities. . . .

– Passy, date uncertain

THE LIGHTER SIDE

THE MOTHER COUNTRY
A Song

We have an old mother that peevish is grown;
She snubs us like children that scarce walk alone;
She forgets we're grown up and have sense of our own;
    Which nobody can deny, deny,
    Which nobody can deny.

If we don't obey orders, whatever the case,
She frowns, and she chides, and she loses all patience,
And sometimes she hits us a slap in the face,
    Which nobody can deny, etc.

Her orders so odd are, we often suspect
That age has impaired her sound intellect;
But still an old mother should have due respect,
    Which nobody can deny, etc.

Let's bear with her humors as well as we can;
But why should we bear the abuse of her man?
When servants make mischief, they earn the rattan,
    Which nobody can deny, etc.

Know too, ye bad neighbors, who aim to divide
The sons from the mother, that still she's our pride;
And if ye attack her we're all of her side,
    Which nobody can deny, etc.

We'll join in her lawsuits, to baffle all those,
Who, to get what she has, will be often her foes;
For we know it must all be our own when she goes,
    Which nobody can deny, deny,
    Which nobody can deny.

        – Written for the *Junto*
        London, probably 1766

ON THE DEATH OF A SQUIRREL

*Franklin had presented a grey squirrel, sent from Phila-
delphia by his wife, to the young daughters of his close
friend, Jonathan Shipley, Bishop of St. Asaph. When their
pet escaped from his cage and was killed by a dog, they
buried him in the garden, and Georgiana Shipley asked
Franklin to compose an epitaph. He responded in the
following letter.*

London, September 26 1772

Dear Miss: I lament with you most sincerely the unfortunate end of poor Mungo. Few squirrels were better ac-
complished; for he had had a good education, had traveled far, and seen much of the world. As he had the honor
of being, for his virtues, your favorite, he should not go,
like common skuggs, without an elegy or an epitaph. Let
us give him one in the monumental style and measure,
which, being neither prose nor verse, is perhaps the prop-
erest for grief; since to use common language would look
as if we were not affected, and to make rhymes would
seem trifling in sorrow.

Epitaph
Alas! poor Mungo!
Happy wert thou, hadst thou known
Thy own felicity.
Remote from the fierce bald eagle,
Tyrant of thy native woods,
Thou hadst nought to fear from his piercing talons,
Nor from the murdering gun
Of the thoughtless sportsman.
Safe in thy wired castle,
Grimalkin could never annoy thee.
Daily wert thou fed with the choicest viands,
By the fair hand of an indulgent mistress

But, discontented,
Thou wouldst have more freedom.
Too soon, alas, didst thou obtain it;
And wandering,
Thou art fallen by the fangs of wanton, cruel Ranger!
Learn hence,
Ye who blindly seek more liberty,
Whether subjects, sons, squirrels, or daughters,
That apparent restraint may be real protection,
Yielding peace and plenty
With security.

You see, my dear Miss, how much more decent and proper this broken style is than if we were to say, by way of epitaph:

Here Skugg
Lies snug
As a bug
In a rug.

And yet there are people in the world of so little feeling as to think that this would be a good enough epitaph for poor Mungo.

THE EPHEMERA

This is the first of Franklin's famous bagatelles, printed in French on his own press at Passy outside Paris, where he lived during his eight and a half years as minister to France. He wrote it in the summer of 1778 for a friend and neighbor, Madame Brillon, wife of a treasury official, in whose house he was a regular and beloved guest.

You may remember, my dear friend, that when we lately spent that happy day in the delightful garden and sweet society of the Moulin Joli*, I stopped a little in one of our walks, and stayed some time behind the company. We had been shown numberless skeletons of a kind of little fly, called an ephemera, whose successive generations, we were told, were bred and expired within the day. I happened to see a living company of them on a leaf, who appeared to be engaged in conversation. You know I understand all the inferior animal tongues. My too great application to the study of them is the best excuse I can give for the little progress I have made in your charming language. I listened through curiosity to the discourse of these little creatures; but as they, in their national vivacity, spoke three or four together, I could make but little of their conversation. I found, however, by some broken expressions that I heard now and then, they were disputing warmly on the merit of two foreign musicians, one a *cousin,* the other a *moscheto*; in which dispute they spent their time, seemingly as regardless of the shortness of life as if they had been sure of living a month. Happy people! thought I; you are certainly under a wise, just, and mild government, since you have no public grievances to complain of, nor any subject of contention but the perfections and imperfections of foreign music. I turned my head from them to an old gray-headed one, who was single on another leaf, and talking to himself. Being amused with his soliloquy, I put it down in writing, in hopes it will likewise amuse her to whom I am so much indebted for the most pleasing of all amusements, her delicious company and heavenly harmony.

"It was," said he, "the opinion of learned philosophers of our race, who lived and flourished long before my time, that this vast world, the Moulin Joli, could not itself subsist more than eighteen hours; and I think there was some foundation for that opinion, since by the apparent motion

* An island in the Seine, part of the country estate of another friend

165

of the great luminary that gives life to all nature, and which in my time has evidently declined considerably towards the ocean at the end of our earth, it must then finish its course, be extinguished in the waters that surround us, and leave the world in cold and darkness necessarily producing universal death and destruction. I have lived seven of those hours, a great age, being no less than four hundred and twenty minutes of time. How very few of us continue so long! I have seen generations born, flourish, and expire. My present friends are the children and grandchildren of the friends of my youth, who are now, alas, no more! And I must soon follow them; for, by the course of nature, though still in health, I cannot expect to live above seven or eight minutes longer. What now avails all my toil and labor in amassing honeydew on this leaf, which I cannot live to enjoy! What the political struggles I have been engaged in for the good of my compatriot inhabitants of this bush, or my philosophical studies for the benefit of our race in general! For in politics what can laws do without morals? Our present race of ephemerae will in a course of minutes become corrupt, like those of other and older bushes, and consequently as wretched. And in philosophy how small our progress! Alas! art is long, and life is short! My friends would comfort me with the idea of a name they say I shall leave behind me, and they tell me I have lived long enough to nature and to glory. But what will fame be to an ephemera who no longer exists? And what will become of all history in the eighteenth hour, when the world itself, even the whole Moulin Joli, shall come to its end and be buried in universal ruin?"

To me, after all my eager pursuits, no solid pleasures now remain but the reflection of a long life spent in meaning well, the sensible conversation of a few good lady ephemerae, and now and then a kind smile and a tune from the ever amiable *Brillante.* . . .

TO MADAME HELVÉTIUS

*The most famous of the "bagatelles" which Franklin printed
at his private press at Passy for the edification of his
friends was written for the widow of the French philosopher Helvétius, another of Franklin's devoted French
friends in whose family circle he spent many gay evenings.
He is believed actually to have proposed to the still-
charming Madame Helvétius; exactly when and how seriously he meant it is not known. The letter was sent and
published in French. The following is the translation
published later by his grandson.*

Mortified at the barbarous resolution pronounced by you
so positively yesterday evening, that you would remain
single the rest of your life as a compliment due to the
memory of your husband, I retired to my chamber. Throwing myself upon my bed, I dreamed that I was dead and
was transported to the Elysian Fields.

I was asked whether I wished to see any persons in particular, to which I replied that I wished to see the philosophers.

"There are two who live here at hand in this garden;
they are good neighbors, and very friendly towards one
another."

"Who are they?"

"Socrates and Helvétius."

"I esteem them both highly, but let me see Helvétius
first, because I understand a little French but not a word
of Greek."

I was conducted to him; he received me with much cour-
tesy, having known me, he said, by character, some time
past. He asked me a thousand questions relative to the
war, the present state of religion, liberty, of the government in France.

"You do not inquire, then," I said, "after your dear

friend, Madame Helvétius; yet she loves you exceedingly; I was in her company not more than an hour ago."

"Ah," said he, "you make me recur to my past happiness, which ought to be forgotten in order to be happy here. For many years I could think of nothing but her; though at length I am consoled. I have taken another wife, the most like her that I could find; she is not indeed altogether so handsome, but she has a great fund of wit and good sense; and her whole study is to please me. She is at this moment gone to fetch the best nectar and ambrosia to regale me; stay here awhile and you will see her."

"I perceive," I said, "that your former friend is more faithful to you than you are to her; she has had several good offers, but has refused them all. I will confess to you that I loved her extremely; but she was cruel to me, and rejected me peremptorily for your sake."

"I pity you sincerely," said he, "for she is an excellent woman, handsome and amiable. But do not the Abbé de la R— and the Abbé M— visit her?"

"Certainly they do; not one of your friends has dropped her acquaintance."

"If you had gained the Abbé M— with a bribe of good coffee and cream, perhaps you would have succeeded, for he is as deep a reasoner as Duns Scotus or St. Thomas; he arranges and methodizes his arguments in such a manner that they are irresistible. Or, if by a fine edition of some old classic you had gained the Abbé de la R— to speak *against* you, that would have been still better, as I always observed that when he recommended anything to her she had a great inclination to do directly the contrary."

As he finished these words the new Madame Helvétius entered with the nectar, and I recognized her immediately as my former American friend, Mrs. Franklin! I reclaimed her, but she answered me coldly: "I was a good wife to you for forty-nine years and four months, nearly half a century; let that content you. I have formed a new connection here which will last to eternity."

Indignant at this refusal of my Eurydice, I immediately resolved to quit those ungrateful shades and return to this good world again, to behold the sun and you! Here I am; let us *avenge ourselves!*

DRINKING SONG

To the Abbé de la Roche*, at Auteuil

I have run over, my dear friend, the little book of poetry by M. Helvétius with which you presented me. The poem on *Happiness* pleased me much, and brought to my recollection a little drinking song which I wrote forty years ago upon the same subject, and which is nearly on the same plan with many of the same thoughts, but very concisely expressed. It is as follows:

Singer
Fair Venus calls; her voice obey,
In beauty's arms spend night and day.
The joys of love all joys excel,
And loving's certainly doing well.

> *Chorus*
> Oh! no!
> Not so!
> For honest souls know,
> Friends and a bottle still bear the bell.

Singer
Then let us get money, like bees lay up honey;
We'll build us new hives, and store each cell.
The sight of our treasure shall yield us great pleasure;
We'll count it and chink it and jingle it well.

* The Abbé was a member of Madame Helvétius's circle at Auteuil. Franklin's letter was originally written in French.

Chorus
Oh! no!
Not so!
For honest souls know,
Friends and a bottle still bear the bell.

Singer
If this does not fit ye, let's govern the city,
In power is pleasure no tongue can tell;
By crowds though you're teased, your pride shall be pleased,
And this can make Lucifer happy in hell!

Chorus
Oh! no!
Not so!
For honest souls know,
Friends and bottle still bear the bell.

Singer
Then toss off your glasses, and scorn the dull asses,
Who missing the kernel still gnaw the shell;
What's love, rule or riches? Wise Solomon teaches,
They're vanity, vanity, vanity, still.

Chorus
That's true;
He knew;
He'd tried them all through;
Friends and bottle still bore the bell.

'Tis a singer, my dear Abbé, who exhorts his companions to seek *happiness* in *love, riches* and in *power.* They reply, singing together, that happiness is not to be found in any of these things; that it is only to be found in *friends* and *wine.* To this proposition the singer at last assents. The phrase *bear the bell* answers to the French *obtain the prize.*

I have often remarked, in reading the works of M. Helvétius, that although we were born and educated in two countries so remote from each other we have often been inspired with the same thoughts; and it is a reflection very flattering to me that we have not only loved the same studies but, as far as we have mutually known them, the same friends, and *the same woman.*

– Passy, date uncertain

IN VINO VERITAS

To the Abbé Morellet

You have often enlivened me, my dear friend, by your excellent drinking songs; in return I beg to edify you by some Christian, moral, and philosophical reflections upon the same subject.

In vino veritas, says the wise man – *Truth is in wine.* Before the days of Noah then, men, having nothing but water to drink, could not discover the truth. Thus they went astray, became abominably wicked, and were justly exterminated by *water,* which they loved to drink.

The good man Noah, seeing that through this pernicious beverage all his contemporaries had perished, took it in aversion; and, to quench his thirst God created the vine and revealed to him the means of converting its fruit into wine. By means of this liquor he discovered numberless important truths; so that ever since his time the word *to divine* has been in common use, signifying originally *to discover by means of* WINE....

Since that time, all things of peculiar excellence, even the Deities themselves, have been called *Divine or Divinities.*

We hear of the conversion of water into wine at the marriage in Cana, as of a miracle. But this conversion is through the goodness of God made every day before our eyes. Behold the rain which descends from heaven upon our vineyards and which incorporates itself with the grapes

171

to be changed into wine; a constant proof that God loves us and loves to see us happy. The miracle in question was only performed to hasten the operation, under circumstances of present necessity which required it.

It is true that God has also instructed man to reduce wine into water. But into what sort of water? – *Water of Life**. And this that man may be able upon occasion to perform the miracle of Cana, and convert common water into that excellent species of wine which we call *punch*.

My Christian brother, be kind and benevolent like God, and do not spoil his good work. He made wine to gladden the heart of man; do not, therefore, when at table you see your neighbor pour wine into his glass, be eager to mingle water with it. Why would you drown truth? It is probable that your neighbor knows better than you can what suits him. Perhaps he does not like water; perhaps he would only put in a few drops for fashion's sake; perhaps he does not wish anyone to observe how much he puts in his glass. Do not then offer water except to children; 'tis a mistaken piece of politeness, and often very inconvenient. I give you this hint as a man of the world; and I will finish as I began, like a good Christian, in making a religious observation of high importance, taken from the Holy Scriptures; I mean that the apostle Paul counseled Timothy very seriously to put wine into his water for the sake of his health; but that not one of the apostles or holy fathers ever recommended *putting water to wine*.

B. F.

P. S. To confirm still more your piety and gratitude to Divine Providence, reflect upon the situation which it has given to the *elbow*. You see in animals who are intended to drink the waters that flow upon the earth, that if they have long legs they have also a long neck, so that they can get at their drink without kneeling down. But man, who was destined to drink wine, is framed in a manner that he may raise the glass to his mouth. If the elbow had been placed

* Eau de vie, that is, brandy

nearer the hand, the part in advance would have been too short to bring the glass up to the mouth; and if it had been nearer the shoulder, that part would have been so long that when it attempted to carry the wine to the mouth it would have overshot the mark, and gone beyond the head; thus, either way, we should have been in the case of Tantalus. But from the actual situation of the elbow we are enabled to drink at our ease, the glass going directly to the mouth. Let us, then, with glass in hand, adore this benevolent wisdom; let us adore and drink!

Passy, undated

THE MORALS OF CHESS

Franklin was a passionate chess player, capable of playing all night through. He relates in his Autobiography that in 1733, when he had mastered the French language and was learning Italian, "an acquaintance who was also learning it used often to tempt me to play chess with him. Finding this took up too much of the time I had to spare for study, I at length refused to play any more unless on this condition, that the victor in every game should have a right to impose a task, either in parts of the grammar to be got by heart or in translations, etc., which tasks the vanquished was to perform, upon honor, before our next meeting. As we played pretty equally, we thus beat one another into that language."

The following was written "to correct (among a few young friends) some little improprieties" in the practice of chess. He told his friend Madame Brillon that it was based on her "generous and magnanimous" way of playing.

The game of chess is not merely an idle amusement. Several very valuable qualities of the mind, useful in the course of human life, are to be acquired or strengthened by it so as to become habits, ready on all occasions. For life is a kind of chess in which we have often points to gain and competitors or adversaries to contend with, and in which there is a vast variety of good and evil events that are in some degree the effects of prudence or the want of it. By playing at chess, then, we may learn, *Foresight,* which looks a little into futurity, and considers the consequences that may attend an action; for it is continually occurring to the player, "If I move this piece, what will be the advantage of my new situation? What use can my adversary make of it to annoy me? What other moves can I make to support it, and to defend myself from his attacks?"

Circumspection, which surveys the whole chessboard, or scene of action; the relations of the several pieces and situations, the dangers they are respectively exposed to, the several possibilities of their aiding each other, the probabilities that the adversary may make this or that move, and attack this or the other piece, and what different means can be used to avoid his stroke or turn its consequences against him.

Caution, not to make our moves too hastily. This habit is best acquired by observing strictly the laws of the game; such as, "If you touch a piece, you must move it somewhere; if you set it down, you must let it stand"; and it is therefore best that these rules should be observed, as the game thereby becomes more the image of human life, and particularly of war; in which, if you have incautiously put yourself into a bad and dangerous position, you cannot obtain your enemy's leave to withdraw your troops and place them more securely, but you must abide all the consequences of your rashness.

And lastly, we learn by chess the habit of *not being discouraged by present appearances in the state of our affairs,* the habit of *hoping for a favorable change,* and that of *persevering in the search of resources.* The game is so full of events, there is such a variety of turns in it, the fortune of it is so subject to sudden vicissitudes, and one so frequently, after long contemplation, discovers the means of extricating one's self from a supposed insurmountable difficulty, that one is encouraged to continue the contest to the last, in hopes of victory by our own skill or at least of getting a stalemate by the negligence of our adversary. And whoever considers what in chess he often sees instances of, that particular pieces of success are apt to produce presumption, and its consequent inattention by which the losses may be recovered, will learn not to be too much discouraged by the present success of his adversary, nor to despair of final good fortune upon every little check he receives in the pursuit of it. . . .

– Passy, 1779

DIALOGUE BETWEEN FRANKLIN AND THE GOUT

Midnight, October 22 1780

Franklin   Eh! Oh! Eh! What have I done to merit these cruel sufferings?

Gout   Many things; you have ate and drank too freely, and too much indulged those legs of yours in their indolence.

Franklin   Who is it that accuses me?

Gout   It is I, even I, the Gout.

Franklin   What! my enemy in person?

Gout   No, not your enemy.

Franklin   I repeat it; my enemy; for you would not only torment my body to death, but ruin my good name; you reproach me as a glutton and a tippler; now all the world, that knows me, will allow that I am neither the one nor the other.

Gout   The world may think as it pleases; it is always very complaisant to itself, and sometimes to its friends; but I very well know that the quantity of meat

175

and drink proper for a man, who takes a reasonable degree of exercise, would be too much for another, who never takes any.

Franklin I take – Eh! Oh! – as much exercise – Eh! – as I can, Madam Gout. You know my sedentary state, and on that account, it would seem, Madam Gout, as if you might spare me a little, seeing it is not altogether my own fault.

Gout Not a jot; your rhetoric and your politeness are thrown away; your apology avails nothing. If your situation in life is a sedentary one, your amusements, your recreations, at least, should be active. You ought to walk or ride; or, if the weather prevents that, play at billiards. But let us examine your course of life. While the mornings are long, and you have leisure to go abroad, what do you do? Why, instead of gaining an appetite for breakfast, by salutary exercise, you amuse yourself, with books, pamphlets, or newspapers, which commonly are not worth the reading. Yet you eat an inordinate breakfast, four dishes of tea, with cream, and one or two buttered toasts, with slices of hung beef, which I fancy are not things the most easily digested. Immediately afterward you sit down to write at your desk, or converse with persons who apply to you on business. Thus the time passes till one, without any kind of bodily exercise. But all this I could pardon, in regard, as you say, to your sedentary condition. But what is your practice after dinner? Walking in the beautiful gardens of those friends, with whom you have dined, would be the choice of men of sense; yours is to be fixed down to chess, where you are found engaged for two or three hours! This is your perpetual recreation, which is the least eligible of any for a sedentary man... If it was in some nook or alley in Paris, deprived of walks, that you played awhile at chess after dinner, this might be excusable; but the same taste prevails with you in Passy, Auteuil, Montmartre, or Sanoy, places where there are the finest gardens and walks, a pure air, beautiful women, and most agreeable and instructive conversation; all which you might enjoy by frequenting the walks. But these are rejected for this abominable game of chess. Fie, then Mr. Franklin! But amidst my instructions, I had almost forgot to administer my wholesome corrections; so take that twinge – and that.

Franklin Oh! Eh! Oh! Ohhh! As much instruction as you please, Madam Gout, and as many reproaches; but pray, Madam, a truce with your corrections!

Gout   No, Sir, no, – I will not abate a particle of what is so much for your good, – therefore –

Franklin Oh! Ehhh! – It is not fair to say I take no exercise, when I do very often, going out to dine and returning in my carriage.

Gout   That, of all imaginable exercises, is the most slight and insignificant, if you allude to the motion of a carriage suspended on springs. By observing the degree of heat obtained by different kinds of motion, we may form an estimate of the quantity of exercise given by each. Thus, for example, if you turn out to walk in winter with cold feet, in an hour's time you will be in a glow all over; ride on horseback, the same effect will scarcely be perceived by four hours' round trotting; but if you loll in a carriage, such as you have mentioned, you may travel all day, and gladly enter the last inn to warm your feet by a fire. Flatter yourself then no longer, that half an hour's airing in your carriage deserves the name of exercise. Providence has appointed few to roll in carriages, while he has given to all a pair of legs, which are machines infinitely more commodious and serviceable. Be grateful, then, and make a proper use of yours. . . Behold your fair friend at Auteuil; a lady who received from bounteous nature more really useful science, than half a dozen such pretenders to philosophy as you have been able to extract from all your books. When she honors you with a visit, it is on foot. She walks all hours of the day, and leaves indolence, and its concomitant maladies, to be endured by her horses. In this see at once the preservative of her health and personal charms.

But when you go to Auteuil, you must have your carriage, though it is no further from Passy to Auteuil than from Auteuil to Passy.

Franklin Your reasonings grow very tiresome.

Gout I stand corrected. I will be silent and continue my office; take that, and that.

Franklin Oh! Ohh! Talk on, I pray you!

Gout No, no; I have a number of twinges for you tonight, and you may be sure of more tomorrow.

Franklin What, with such a fever! I shall go distracted. Oh! Eh! Can no one bear it for me?

Gout Ask that of your horses; they have served you faithfully.

Franklin How can you so cruelly sport with my torments?

Gout Sport! I am very serious. I have here a list of offences against your own health distinctly written, and can justify every stroke inflicted on you.

Franklin Read it then.

Gout It is too long a detail; but I will briefly mention some particulars.

Franklin Proceed. I am all attention.

Gout Do you remember how often you have promised yourself, the following morning, a walk in the grove of Boulogne, in the garden de la Muette, or in your own garden, and have violated your promise, alleging, at one time, it was too cold, at another too warm, too windy, too moist, or what else you pleased; when in truth it was too nothing, but your insuperable love of ease?

Franklin That I confess may have happened occasionally, probably ten times in a year.

Gout Your confession is very far short of the truth; the gross amount is one hundred and ninety-nine times.

Franklin Is it possible?

Gout So possible, that it is fact; you may rely on the accuracy of my statement. You know M. Brillon's gardens, and what fine walks they contain; you know the handsome flight of a hundred steps, which lead from the terrace above to the lawn below. You have been in the practice of visiting this amiable family twice a week, after dinner, and it is a maxim of your own, that "a man may take as much exercise in walking a mile, up and down stairs, as in ten on level ground." What an opportunity was here for you to have had exercise in both these ways! Did you embrace it – and how often?

Franklin I cannot immediately answer that question.

Gout I will do it for you; not once.

Franklin Not once?

Gout Even so. During the summer you went there at six o'clock. You found the charming lady, with her lovely children and friends, eager to walk with you, and entertain you with their agreeable conversation; and what has been your choice? Why to sit on the terrace, satisfying yourself with the fine prospect, and passing your eye over the beauties of the garden below, without taking one step to descend and walk about in them. On the contrary, you call for tea and the chessboard; and lo! you are occupied in your seat till nine o'clock, and that besides two hours' play after dinner; and then, instead of walking home, which would have bestirred you a little, you step into your carriage. How absurd to suppose that all this carelessness can be reconcilable with health, without my interposition!

Franklin I am convinced now of the justness of poor Richard's remark, that "our debts and our sins are always greater than we think for."

Gout So it is. You philosophers are sages in your maxims, and fools in your conduct.

Franklin But do you charge among my crimes, that I return in a carriage from M. Brillon's?

Gout Certainly; for, having been seated all the while, you cannot object the fatigue of the day, and cannot want therefore the relief of a carriage.

Franklin What then would you have me do with my carriage?

Gout   Burn it if you choose; you would at least get heat out of it once in this way; or, if you dislike that proposal, here's another for you; observe the poor peasants, who work in the vineyards and grounds about the villages of Passy, Auteuil, Chaillot, &c.; you may find every day, among these deserving creatures, four or five old men and women, bent and perhaps crippled by weight of years, and too long and too great labor. After a most fatiguing day, these people have to trudge a mile or two to their smoky huts. Order your coachman to set them down. This is an act that will be good for your soul; and, at the same time, after your visit to the Brillons, if you return on foot, that will be good for your body.

Franklin   Ah! how tiresome you are!

Gout   Well, then, to my office; it should not be forgotten that I am your physician. There.

Franklin   Ohhh! what a devil of a physician!

Gout   How ungrateful you are to say so! Is it not I who, in the character of your physician, have saved you from the palsy, dropsy, and apoplexy? one or other of which would have done for you long ago, but for me.

Franklin   I submit, and thank you for the past, but entreat the discontinuance of your visits for the future; for, in my mind, one had better die than be cured so dolefully. Permit me just to hint, that I have also not been unfriendly to *you*. I never feed physician or quack of any kind, to enter the list against you; if then you do not leave me to my repose, it may be said you are ungrateful too.

Gout   I can scarcely acknowledge that as any objection. As to quacks, I despise them; they may kill you indeed, but cannot injure me. And, as to regular physicians, they are at last convinced that the gout, in such a subject as you are, is no disease, but a remedy; and wherefore cure a remedy? – but to our business, – there.

Franklin   Oh! oh! – for Heaven's sake leave me! and I promise faithfully never more to play at chess, but to take exercise daily, and live temperately.

Gout   I know you too well. You promise fair; but, after a few months of good health, you will return to your old habits; your fine promises will be forgotten like the forms of last year's clouds. Let us then finish the account, and I will go. But I leave you with an assurance of visiting you again at a proper time and place; for my object is your good, and you are sensible now that I am your *real friend*.

PROPOSED NEW VERSION OF THE BIBLE

It is now more than one hundred and seventy years since the translation of our common English Bible. The language in that time is much changed, and the style being obsolete, and thence less agreeable, is perhaps one reason why the reading of that excellent book is of late so much neglected. I have therefore thought it would be well to procure a new version in which, preserving the sense, the turn of phrase and manner of expression should be modern. I do not pretend to have the necessary abilities for such a work myself; I throw out the hint for the consideration of the learned and only venture to send you a few verses of the first chapter of Job, which may serve as a sample of the kind of version I would recommend.

OLD TEXT

Verse 6. Now there was a day when the sons of God came to present themselves before the Lord, and Satan came also amongst them.

7. And the Lord said unto Satan, Whence comest thou? Then Satan answered the

NEW VERSION

Verse 6. And it being *levee* day in heaven, all God's nobility came to court, to present themselves before him; and Satan also appeared in the circle, as one of the ministry.

7. And God said to Satan, You have been some time absent; where were you?

Lord, and said, From going to and fro in the earth, and from walking up and down in it.

8. And the Lord said unto Satan, Hast thou considered my servant Job, that there is none like him in the earth, a perfect and an upright man, one that feareth God, and escheweth evil?

9. Then Satan answered the Lord, and said, Doth Job fear God for naught?

10. Hast thou not made an hedge about his house, and about all that he hath on every side? Thou hast blessed the work of his hands, and his substance is increased in the land.

11. But put forth thine hand now, and touch all that he hath, and he will curse thee to thy face.

And Satan answered, I have been at my country-seat, and in different places visiting my friends.

8. And God said, Well, what think you of Lord Job? You see he is my best friend, a perfectly honest man, full of respect for me, and avoiding every thing that might offend me.

9. And Satan answered, Does your Majesty imagine that his good conduct is the effect of mere personal attachment and affection?

10. Have you not protected him, and heaped your benefits upon him, till he is grown enormously rich?

11. Try him; – only withdraw your favor, turn him out of his places, and withhold his pensions, and you will soon find him in the opposition.

– From a letter to the Printer of ——— Passy, 1781

STATESMAN AT HOME

I agree with you perfectly in your disapprobation of war. Abstracted from the inhumanity of it, I think it wrong in point of human prudence; for whatever advantage one nation would obtain from another, whether it be part of their territory, the liberty of commerce with them, free passage on their rivers, etc., etc., it would be much cheaper to purchase such advantage with ready money than to pay the expense of acquiring it by war.

An army is a devouring monster, and when you have raised it you have, in order to subsist it, not only the fair charges of pay, clothing, provisions, arms, and ammunition, with numberless other contingent and just charges, to answer and satisfy, but you have all the additional knavish charges of the numerous tribe of contractors to defray, with those of every other dealer who furnishes the articles wanted for your army, and takes advantage of that want to demand exorbitant prices.

It seems to me that if statesmen had a little more arithmetic, or were more accustomed to calculation, wars would be much less frequent.

I am confident that Canada might have been purchased from France for a tenth part of the money England spent in the conquest of it.

And if, instead of fighting with us for the power of taxing us, she had kept us in good humor by allowing us to dispose of our own money, and now and then giving us a little of hers, by way of donation to colleges, or hospitals, or for cutting canals, or fortifying ports, she might have easily drawn from us much more by our occasional voluntary grants and contributions than ever she could by taxes.

Sensible people will give a bucket or two of water to a dry pump, that they may afterward get from it all they have occasion for. Her ministry were deficient in that little point of common sense. And so they spent one hundred millions of her money, and after all lost what they contended for.

– From a letter to Jane Mecom, Franklin's sister
Philadelphia, September 20 1787

SPEECH TO THE CONSTITUTIONAL CONVENTION

The Constitutional Convention met in Philadelphia throughout the summer of 1787 to draw up the first Constitution for the newly created United States. Franklin, in his eighty-third year, was the oldest delegate, and with the wisdom of years behind him he used his influence to achieve agreement rather than press for his ideas. None of his own proposals – for a single legislature, a plural executive, and public officials who would serve for the honor, without salary – was adopted. He was the author of the compromise according to which states are represented in the House of Representatives according to population but have an equal voice in the Senate. His last speech, made on the final day, September 17, was considered the literary masterpiece of the Convention.

Mr. President: I confess that there are several parts of this Constitution which I do not at present approve, but I am not sure I shall never approve them; for, having lived long, I have experienced many instances of being obliged, by better information or fuller consideration, to change opinions even on important subjects which I once thought right, but found to be otherwise. It is therefore that the older I grow, the more apt I am to doubt my own judgment, and to pay more respect to the judgment of others. Most men indeed, as well as most sects in religion, think them-

185

selves in possession of all truth, and that wherever others differ from them, it is so far error. Steele, a Protestant, in a dedication tells the Pope that the only difference between our churches in their opinions of the certainty of their doctrines is, the Church of Rome is infallible, and the Church of England is never in the wrong. But though many private persons think almost as highly of their own infallibility as of that of their sect, few express it so naturally as a certain French lady who in a dispute with her sister, said:

"I don't know how it happens, Sister, but I meet with nobody but myself that is *always* in the right" – *Il n'y a que moi qui a toujours raison.*

In these sentiments, Sir, I agree to this Constitution, with all its faults, if they are such; because I think a general government necessary for us, and there is no form of government but what may be a blessing to the people if well administered; and I believe farther that this is likely to be well administered for a course of years, and can only end in despotism, as other forms have done before it, when the people shall become so corrupted as to need despotic government, being incapable of any other. I doubt too whether any other Convention we can obtain may be able to make a better Constitution. For when you assemble a number of men to have the advantage of their joint wisdom, you inevitably assemble with those men all their prejudices, their passions, their errors of opinion, their local interests, and their selfish views. From such an assembly can a perfect production be expected? It therefore astonishes me, Sir, to find this system approaching so near to perfection as it does; and I think it will astonish our enemies, who are waiting with confidence to hear that our counsels are confounded like those of the builders of Babel; and that our States are on the point of separation only to meet hereafter for the purpose of cutting one another's throats. Thus I consent, Sir, to this Constitution because I expect no better, and because I am not sure that it is not the best. The opinions I have had of its errors I sacrifice to the public good. I have never whispered a syllable of them abroad. Within these walls they were born, and here they shall die. If every one of us, in returning to our constituents, were to report the objections he has had to it, and endeavor to gain partisans in support of them, we might prevent its being generally received, and thereby lose all the salutary effects and great advantages resulting naturally in our favor among foreign nations, as well as among ourselves, from our real or apparent unanimity. Much of the strength and efficiency of any government in procuring and securing happiness to the people, depends on opinion, on the general opinion, of the goodness of the government, as well as of the wisdom and integrity of its governors.

I hope therefore that for our own sakes, as a part of the people, and for the sake of our posterity, we shall act heartily and unanimously in recommending this Constitution (if approved by Congress and confirmed by the Conventions) wherever our influence may extend, and turn our future thoughts and endeavors to the means of having it well administered.

On the whole, Sir, I cannot help expressing a wish that every member of the Convention who may still have objections to it would with me on this occasion doubt a little of his own infallibility, and, to make manifest our unanimity, put his name to this instrument.

WHY SHOULD PROPERTY BE REPRESENTED AT ALL?

In Franklin firm belief in the rights of men as opposed to those of wealth and privilege did not weaken with age. In November, 1789, he opposed a plan to alter the Constitution of his home state of Pennsylvania so that the upper house of the state legislature would be chosen by those owning one thousand pounds worth of property, while the lower would represent the ordinary taxpayer.

Several questions may arise upon this proposition. First, what is the proportion of freemen possessing lands and houses of one thousand pounds' value compared to that of freemen whose possessions are inferior? Are they as one to ten? Are they even as one to twenty? I should doubt whether they are as one to fifty. If this minority is to choose a body expressly to control that which is to be chosen by the great majority of the freemen, what have this great majority done to forfeit so great a portion of their right in elections? Why is this power of control, contrary to the spirit of all democracies, to be vested in a minority instead of a majority? Then, is it intended, or is it not, that the rich should have a vote in the choice of members for the Lower House, while those of inferior property are deprived of the right of voting for members of the Upper House? And why should the Upper House, chosen by a minority, have equal power with the Lower chosen by a majority? Is it supposed that wisdom is the necessary concomitant of riches, and that one man worth a thousand pounds must have as much wisdom as twenty who have each only nine hundred and ninety-nine; and why is property to be represented at all? Suppose one of our Indian nations should now agree to form a civil society; each individual would bring into the stock of the society little more property than his gun and his blanket, for at present he has no other. We know that when one of them has attempted to keep a few swine he has not been able to maintain a property in them, his neighbors thinking they have a right to kill and eat them whenever they want provision, it being one of their maxims that hunting is free for all; the accumulation, therefore, of property in such a society must be an effect of the protection afforded to it by the joint strength of the society in the execution of its laws.

Private property, therefore, is a creature of society, and is subject to the calls of that society whenever its necessities shall require it, even to its last farthing; its contributions to the public exigences are not to be considered as conferring a benefit on the public, entitling the contributors to the distinction of honor and power, but as the return of an obligation previously received, or the payment of a just debt. The combinations of civil society are not like those of a set of merchants who club their property in different proportions for building and freighting a ship and may therefore have some right to vote in the disposition of the voyage in a greater or less degree according to their respective contributions; but the important ends of civil society, and the personal securities of life and liberty there, remain the same in every member of the society; and the poorest continues to have an equal claim to them with the most opulent, whatever difference time, chance, or industry may occasion in their circumstances.

On these considerations, I am sorry to see the signs ... of a disposition among some of our people to commence an aristocracy by giving the rich a predominancy in government.

> – From *Queries and Remarks Respecting Alterations in the Constitution of Pennsylvania*
> 1789

ANTI-SLAVERY SEEDS

Dear Friend: ... I wish success to your endeavors for obtaining an abolition of the Slave Trade. The epistle from your Yearly Meeting for the year 1758 was not the *first sowing* of the good seed you mention; for I find by an old pamphlet in my possession that George Keith, near a hundred years since, wrote a paper against the practice, said to be "given forth by the appointment of the meeting held by him at Philip James's house in the city of Philadelphia, about the year 1693*"; wherein a strict charge was given to Friends "that they should set their Negroes at liberty after some reasonable time of service, etc. etc." And about the year 1728 or 1729 I myself printed a book for Ralph Sandyford, another of your Friends in this city, against keeping Negroes in slavery; two editions of which he distributed gratis. And about the year 1736 I printed another book on the same subject for Benjamin Lay, who also professed being one of your Friends, and he distributed the books chiefly among them. By these instances it appears that the seed was indeed sown in the good ground of your profession, though much earlier than the time you mention, and its springing up to effect at last, though so late, is some confirmation of Lord Bacon's observation that *a good motion never dies;* and it may encourage us in making such, though hopeless of their taking immediate effect. . . .

– From a letter to John Wright, London
dated Philadelphia, November 4 1789

A PRO-SLAVERY PARODY

Slavery was the last public matter with which Franklin concerned himself. The first American society for the abolition of slavery had been founded in Pennsylvania in 1775. It had discontinued its activity during the war, but renewed its efforts in 1787, with Franklin as president. In that capacity he signed an appeal to the public for funds in November, 1789. In February of the same year he had put his signature to a memorial from the society to the

---

* Herbert Aptheker in *And Why Not Every Man?* (Seven Seas Books, Berlin, 1961) attributed the first collective anti-slavery protest to four Quakers who submitted a statement to their Meeting in Germantown, Pennsylvania, on February 18 1688.

First Congress, urging it to act to discourage slavery. In March, 1790, less than a month before his death, he wrote his famous Pro-Slavery Parody for the Federal Gazette in which he ridiculed the pro-slavery arguments delivered during the debate which ended in the rejection of this memorial.

To the Editor of the Federal Gazette

Reading last night in your excellent paper the speech of Mr. Jackson in Congress against their meddling with the affair of slavery, or attempting to mend the condition of the slaves, it put me in mind of a similar one made about one hundred years since by Sidi Mehemet Ibrahim, a member of the Divan of Algiers, which may be seen in Martin's Account of his Consulship, anno 1687. It was against granting the petition of the sect called Erika, or Purists, who prayed for the abolition of piracy and slavery as being unjust. Mr. Jackson does not quote it; perhaps he has not seen it. If, therefore, some of its reasonings are to be found in his eloquent speech, it may only show that men's interests and intellects operate and are operated on with surprising similarity in all countries and climates, when under similar circumstances. The African's speech, as translated, is as follows.

Allah Bismillah, etc. God is great, and Mahomet is his Prophet.

"Have these *Erika* considered the consequences of granting their petition? If we cease our cruises against the Christians, how shall we be furnished with the commodities their countries produce, and which are so necessary for us? If we forbear to make slaves of their people, who in this hot climate are to cultivate our lands? Who are to perform the common labors of our city, and in our families? Must we not then be our own slaves? And is there not

191

more compassion and more favor due to us as Mussulmen, than to these Christian dogs?

"We have now above 50 000 slaves in and near Algiers. This number, if not kept up by fresh supplies, will soon diminish, and be gradually annihilated. If we then cease taking and plundering the infidel ships, and making slaves of the seamen and passengers, our lands will become of no value for want of cultivation; the rents of houses in the city will sink one half; and the revenues of government arising from its share of prizes be totally destroyed! And for what? To gratify the whims of a whimsical sect, who would have us not only forbear making more slaves, but even to manumit those we have.

"But who is to indemnify their masters for the loss? Will the state do it? Is our treasury sufficient? Will the *Erika* do it? Can they do it? Or would they, to do what they think justice to the slaves, do a greater injustice to the owners? And if we set our slaves free, what is to be done with them? Few of them will return to their countries; they know too well the greater hardships they must there be subject to; they will not embrace our holy religion; they will not adopt our manners; our people will not pollute themselves by intermarrying with them. Must we maintain them as beggars in our streets, or suffer our properties to be the prey of their pillage? For men long accustomed to slavery will not work for a livelihood when not compelled. And what is there so pitiable in their present condition? Were they not slaves in their own countries.

"Are not Spain, Portugal, France, and the Italian states governed by despots, who hold their subjects in slavery, without exception? Even England treats its sailors as slaves; for they are, whenever the government pleases, seized and confined in ships of war, condemned not only to work, but to fight, for small wages, or a mere subsistence, not better than our slaves are allowed by us. Is their condition then made worse by their falling into our hands?

No; they have only exchanged one slavery for another, and I may say a better; for here they are brought into a land where the sun of Islamism gives forth its light, and shines in full splendor, and they have an opportunity of making themselves acquainted with the true doctrine, and thereby saving their immortal souls. Those who remain at home have not that happiness. Sending the slaves home then would be sending them out of light into darkness.

"I repeat the question: What is to be done with them? I have heard it suggested that they may be planted in the wilderness, where there is plenty of land for them to subsist on, and where they may flourish as a free state; but they are, I doubt, too little disposed to labor without compulsion, as well as too ignorant to establish a good government, and the wild Arabs would soon molest and destroy or again enslave them. While serving us, we take care to provide them with every thing, and they are treated with humanity. The laborers in their own country are, as I am well informed, worse fed, lodged and clothed. The condition of most of them is therefore already mended, and requires no further improvement. Here their lives are in safety. They are not liable to be impressed for soldiers, and forced to cut one another's Christian throats, as in the wars of their own countries. If some of the religious mad bigots, who now tease us with their silly petitions, have in a fit of blind zeal freed their slaves, it was not generosity, it was not humanity, that moved them to the action; it was from the conscious burden of a load of sins, and hope, from the supposed merits of so good a work, to be excused of damnation.

"How grossly are they mistaken in imagining slavery to be disallowed by the *Alcoran*! Are not the two precepts, to quote no more, *Masters, treat your slaves with kindness; Slaves, serve your masters with cheerfulness and fidelity*, clear proofs to the contrary? Nor can the plundering of infidels be in that sacred book forbidden, since it is well known from it that God has given the world, and all that it contains, to his faithful Mussulmen, who are to enjoy it of right as fast as they conquer it. Let us then hear no more of this detestable proposition, the manumission of Christian slaves, the adoption of which would, by depreciating our lands and houses, and thereby depriving so many good citizens of their properties, create universal discontent, and provoke insurrections, to the endangering of government and producing general confusion. I have therefore no doubt, but this wise council will prefer the comfort and happiness of a whole nation of true believers to the whim of a few *Erika,* and dismiss their petition."

The result was, as Martin tells us, that the Divan came to this resolution: "The doctrine, that plundering and enslaving the Christians is unjust, is at best *problematical*; but that it is in the interest of this state to continue the practice is clear; therefore let the petition be rejected."

And it was rejected accordingly.

And since like motives are apt to produce in the minds of men like opinions and resolutions, may we not venture to predict from this account, that the petitions to the Parliament of England for abolishing the slave trade, to say nothing of other legislatures, and the debates upon them, will have a similar conclusion. . . .

PROVISION FOR THE FUTURE

Franklin's high principles and keen business sense are nowhere better illustrated than in the codicil to his will, in which he tried to anticipate the needs of his two native cities, Boston and Philadelphia, two centuries hence.

It having long been a fixed political opinion of mine that in a democratic state there ought to be no offices of profit, for the reasons I had given in an article of my drawing in our Constitution, it was my intention when I accepted the

194

office of President* to devote the appointed salary to some public uses. Accordingly I had already, before I made my will in July last, given large sums of it to colleges, schools, building of churches, etc.; and in that will I bequeathed two thousand pounds more to the State for the purpose of making the Schuylkill navigable. But understanding since that such a sum will do but little towards accomplishing such a work, and that the project is not likely to be undertaken for many years to come, and having entertained another idea that I hope may be more extensively useful, I do hereby revoke and annul that bequest, and direct that the certificates I have for what remains due to me of the salary be sold towards raising the sum of two thousand pounds sterling, to be disposed of as I am now about to order.

It has been an opinion that he who receives an estate from his ancestors is under some kind of obligation to transmit the same to their posterity. This obligation does not lie on me, who never inherited a shilling from any ancestor or relation. I shall, however, if it is not diminished by some accident before my death, leave a considerable estate among my descendants and relations. The above observation is made merely as some apology to my family for making bequests that do not appear to have any immediate relation to their advantage.

I was born in Boston, New England, and owe my first instructions in literature to the free grammar schools established there. I have therefore already considered these schools in my will. But I am also under obligation to the State of Massachusetts for having, unasked, appointed me formerly their agent in England, with a handsome salary, which continued for some years. . . .

I have considered that, among artisans, good apprentices are most likely to make good citizens, and having

* After his return from France, Franklin was three times unanimously elected President of Pennsylvania.

myself been bred to a manual art, printing, in my native town, and afterwards assisted to set up my business in Philadelphia by kind loans of money from two friends there, which was the foundation of my fortune and of all the utility in life that may be ascribed to me, I wish to be useful even after my death, if possible, in forming and advancing other young men that may be serviceable to their country in both those towns. To this end I devote two thousand pounds sterling, of which I give one thousand thereof to the inhabitants of the town of Boston, in Massachusetts. . . .

And, as it is presumed that there will always be found in Boston virtuous and benevolent citizens, willing to bestow a part of their time in doing good to the rising generation by superintending and managing this institution gratis, it is hoped that no part of the money will at any time be dead or be diverted to other purposes, but be continually augmented by the interest; in which case there may, in time, be more than the occasions in Boston shall require, and then some may be spared to the neighboring or other towns. . . .

If this plan is executed, and succeeds as projected without interruption for one hundred years, the sum will then be one hundred and thirty-one thousand pounds; of which I would have the managers of the donation to the town of Boston then lay out, at their discretion, one hundred thousand pounds in public works which may be judged to be of most general utility to the inhabitants. . . The remaining thirty-one thousand pounds I would have continued to be let out on interest, in the manner above directed, for another hundred years, as I hope it will have been found that the institution has had a good effect on the conduct of youth and been of service to many worthy characters and useful citizens.

At the end of this second term, if no unfortunate accident has prevented the operation, the sum will be four million and sixty-one thousand pounds sterling*, of which I leave one million sixty-one thousand pounds to the disposition of the inhabitants of the town of Boston, and three millions to the disposition of the government of the State. . . .

All the directions herein given respecting the disposition and management of the donation to the inhabitants of Boston I would have observed respecting that to the inhabitants of Philadelphia. . . . I recommend that at the end of the first hundred years, if not done before, the corporation of the city employ a part of the hundred thousand pounds in bringing, by pipes, the water of Wissakickon Creek into the town so as to supply the inhabitants, which I apprehend may be done without great difficulty, the level of the creek being much above that of the city and may be made higher by a dam. I also recommend making the Schuylkill completely navigable. . . .

Considering the accidents to which all human affairs and projects are subject in such a length of time, I have, perhaps, too much flattered myself with a vain fancy that these dispositions, if carried into execution, will be continued without interruption and have the effects proposed. I hope, however, that if the inhabitants of the two cities should not think fit to undertake the execution they will, at least, accept the offer of these donations as a mark of my good will, a token of my gratitude, and a testimony of my earnest desire to be useful to them after my departure. . . .

> – Codicil to the Last Will and
> Testament of Benjamin Franklin
> Philadelphia, June 23 1789

* In his biography of Benjamin Franklin (Viking Press, New York, 1938) Carl Van Doren reports that in 1907 the Franklin Fund in Philadelphia amounted to $172 350; at the end of the first hundred years the Boston Fund had $391 000, part of which was withdrawn to help build the Franklin Union, an evening technical school. The part which was reinvested had grown to $593 000 in 1935, and by the end of the second hundred years in 1991 is expected to reach four million dollars.

To Josiah Franklin

Honored Father: I have your favors of the 21st of March, in which you both seem concerned lest I have imbibed some erroneous opinions. Doubtless I have my share; and when the natural weakness and imperfection of human understanding is considered, the unavoidable influence of education, custom, books and company upon our ways of thinking, I imagine a man must have a good deal of vanity who believes, and a good deal of boldness who affirms, that all the doctrines he holds are true and all he rejects are false. And perhaps the same may justly be said of every sect, church and society of men, when they assume to themselves that infallibility which they deny to the Pope and councils.

I think opinions should be judged of by their influences and effects; and if a man holds none that tend to make him less virtuous or more vicious, it may be concluded he holds none that are dangerous; which I hope is the case with me.

I am sorry you should have any uneasiness on my account; and if it were a thing possible for one to alter his opinions in order to please another, I know none whom I ought more willingly to oblige in that respect than yourselves. But since it is no more in a man's power to *think* than to *look* like another, methinks all that should be expected from me is to keep my mind open to conviction, to hear patiently and examine attentively whatever is offered to me for that end; and if, after all, I continue in the same errors, I believe your usual charity will induce you rather to pity and excuse than blame me. In the meantime, your care and concern for me is what I am very thankful for.

My mother grieves that one of her sons is an Arian, another an Arminian. What an Arminian or an Arian is, I cannot say that I very well know. The truth is, I make such distinctions very little my study. I think vital religion has always suffered when orthodoxy is more regarded than virtue; and the Scriptures assure me that at the last day we shall not be examined on what we *thought* but what we *did;* and our recommendation will not be that we said *Lord Lord!* but that we did good to our fellow creatures. See Matt. XXV....

To John Franklin

Philadelphia, 1745

Our people are extremely impatient to hear of your success at Cape Breton*. My shop is filled with thirty inquiries at the coming in of every post. Some wonder the place is not yet taken. I tell them I shall be glad to hear that news three months hence. Fortified towns are hard nuts to crack; and your teeth have not been accustomed to it. Taking strong places is a particular trade which you have taken up without serving an apprenticeship to it. Armies and veterans need skilful engineers to direct them in their attack. Have you any? But some seem to think forts are as easy taken as snuff. Father Moody's prayers look tolerably modest. You have a fast and prayer day for that purpose, in which I compute five hundred thousand petitions were offered up to the same effect in New England, which added to the petitions of every family morning and evening, multiplied by the number of days since January 25th, make forty-five millions of prayers; which set against the prayers of a few priests in the garrison to the Virgin Mary give a vast balance in your favor.

If you do not succeed, I fear I shall have but an indifferent opinion of Presbyterian prayers in such cases as long as I live. Indeed, in attacking strong towns I should have more dependence on *works* than on *faith;* for, like the kingdom of heaven, they are to be taken by force and vio-

* John Franklin, Benjamin Franklin's brother, took part in a British expedition against the French in Canada. Cape Breton, Nova Scotia, fell with the surrender of Louisburg on June 17 1745.

lence; and in a French garrison I suppose there are devils of that kind that are not to be cast out by prayers and fasting, unless it be by their own fasting for want of provisions. I believe there is Scripture in what I have wrote, but I cannot adorn the margin with quotations, having a bad memory and no Concordance at hand.

To Catherine Ray

On a trip from Boston to Philadelphia, Franklin met Catherine Ray (later Catherine Ray Greene) and a warm friendship was established between the twenty-three-year-old girl and the fifty-year-old philosopher. Although they saw each other only a few times thereafter, an affectionate correspondence continued between them for thirty-five years.

Philadelphia, September 11 1755

Now it is near four months since I have been favored with a single line from you; but I will not be angry with you, because it is my fault. I ran in debt to you three or four letters, and, as I did not pay, you would not trust me any more, and you had some reason. But, believe me, I am honest, and, though I should never make equal returns, you shall see I will keep fair accounts. Equal returns I can never make, though I should write to you by every post; for the pleasure I receive from one of yours is more than you can have from two of mine. The small news, the domestic occurrences among our friends, the natural pictures you draw of persons, the sensible observations and reflections you make, and the easy, chatty manner in which you express everything, all contribute to heighten the pleasure; and the more as they remind me of those hours and miles that we talked away so agreeably, even in a winter journey, a wrong road, and a soaking shower.

I long to hear whether you have continued ever since

in that monastery; or have broke into the world again, doing pretty mischief; how the lady Wards do, and how many of them are married, or about it; what is become of Mr. B. and Mr. L., and what the state of your heart is at this instant? But that, perhaps, I ought not to know; and therefore I will not conjure, as you sometimes say I do. If I could conjure, it should be to know what was that oddest question about me that ever was thought of, which you tell me a lady had just sent to ask you.

I commend your prudent resolutions, in the article of granting favors to lovers. But if I were courting you, I could not hardly approve such conduct. I should even be malicious enough to say you were too knowing, and tell you the old story of the Girl and the Miller. I enclose you the songs you write for, and with them your Spanish letter with a translation. I honor that honest Spaniard for loving you. It showed the goodness of his taste and judgment. But you must forget him, and bless some worthy young Englishman.

You have spun a long thread, five thousand and twenty-two yards. It will reach almost from Rhode Island hither. I wish I had hold of one end of it, to pull you to me. But you would break it rather than come. The cords of love and friendship are longer and stronger, and in times past have drawn me farther; even back from England to Philadelphia. I guess that some of the same kind will one day draw you out of that Island.

I was extremely pleased with the turf you sent me. The Irish people, who have seen it, say it is the right sort; but I cannot learn that we have anything like it here. The cheeses, particularly one of them, were excellent. All our friends have tasted it, and all agree that it exceeds any English cheese they ever tasted.

Mrs. Franklin was very proud that a young lady should have so much regard for her old husband as to send him such a present. We talk of you every time it comes to table. She is sure you are a sensible girl, and a notable housewife, and talks of bequeathing me to you as a legacy; but I ought to wish you a better, and hope she will live these hundred years; for we are grown old together, and if she has any faults I am so used to them that I don't perceive them; as the song says:

Some faults we have all, and so has my Joan,
But then they're exceedingly small;
And, now I'm used to them, they're just like my own,
I scarcely can see them at all;
My dear friends,
I scarcely can see them at all*.

Indeed, I begin to think she has none, as I think of you. And since she is willing I should love you as much as you are willing to be loved by me, let us join in wishing the old lady a long life and a happy.

With her respectful compliments to you, to your good mother and sisters, present mine, though unknown; and believe me to be, dear girl, your affectionate friend and humble servant. . . .

P.S. Sally says: "Papa, my love to Miss Katy." If it was not quite unreasonable, I should desire you to write to me every post, whether you hear from me or not. As to your spelling, don't let those laughing girls put you out of conceit with it. It is the best in the world, for every letter of it stands for something.

To Mary Stevenson

Philadelphia, March 25 1763

My Dear Polly: Your pleasing favor of November 11th is now before me. It found me, as you supposed it would, happy with my American friends and family about me; and it made me more happy in showing me that I am not

* This is a verse from a song which Franklin wrote for the entertainment of his friends at the *Junto*.

yet forgotten by the dear friends I left in England. And indeed, why should I fear that they will ever forget me when I feel so strongly that I shall ever remember them?....

Of all the enviable things England has, I envy it most its people. Why should that petty island, which compared to America is but like a stepping stone in a brook, scarce enough of it above water to keep one's shoes dry – why, I say – should that little island enjoy in almost every neighborhood more sensible, virtuous and elegant minds that we can collect in ranging a hundred leagues of our vast forests? But it is said the Arts delight to travel westward. You have effectually defended us in this glorious war*, and in time you will improve us. After the first cares for the necessaries of life are over, we shall come to think of the embellishments....

I do not wonder at the behavior you mention of Dr. S— towards me, for I have long since known him thoroughly. I made that man my enemy by doing him too much kindness. It is the honestest way of acquiring an enemy. And since it is convenient to have at least one enemy who, by his readiness to revile one on all occasions may make one careful of one's conduct, I shall keep him an enemy for that purpose....

To Mrs. Deborah Franklin

London, June 4 1765

My Dear Child:... I could have wished to be present at the finishing of the kitchen, as it is a mere machine; and being new to you I think you will scarce know how to

* The "glorious war" ironically referred to here was the Seven Years' War (1756–63), known on the American continent as the French and Indian War. It was highly unpopular in the colonies and the English had difficulty recruiting soldiers. By it Britain acquired Canada from France.

work it; the several contrivances to carry off steam, smell and smoke not being fully explained to you. The oven I suppose was put up by the written directions in my former letter. You mention nothing of the furnace. If that iron one is not set, let it alone till my return, when I shall bring a more convenient copper one. . . .

I cannot but complain in my mind of Mr. Smith, that the house is so long unfit for you to get into, the fences not put up, nor the other necessary articles ready. The well I expected would have been dug in the winter or early in the spring, but I hear nothing of it. You should have gardened long before the date of your last, but it seems the rubbish was not removed. I am much obliged to my good old friends that did me the honor to remember me in the unfinished kitchen. I hope soon to drink with them in the parlour. . . .

It rejoices me to learn that you are more free than you used to be from the headache, and that pain in your side. I am likewise in perfect health. God is very good to us both in many respects. Let us enjoy his favors with a thankful cheerful heart; and as we can make no direct return to him, show our sense of his goodness by continuing to do good to our fellow creatures, whether good or bad. . . .

To Mrs. Deborah Franklin

London, April 6 1766

My Dear Child: As the Stamp Act* is at length repealed, I am willing you should have a new gown, which you may

* The Stamp Act, passed by Parliament in 1765, required the payment of a fee for every legal paper, including newspapers. The colonists considered it an outrage – a tax levied without their consent by a body in which they were not represented. They responded by boycotting British goods. Franklin was instrumental in having the Stamp Act repealed, in February, 1766.

suppose I did not send sooner as I knew you would not like to be finer than your neighbors, unless in a gown of your own spinning. Had the trade between the two countries totally ceased, it was a comfort to me to recollect that I had once been clothed from head to foot in woolen and linen of my wife's manufacture, that I never was prouder of any dress in my life, and that she and her daughter might do it again if it was necessary. I told the Parliament that it was my opinion, before the old clothes of the Americans were worn out, they might have new ones of their own making.

I have sent you a fine piece of Pompadour satin, fourteen yards, cost eleven shillings a yard; a silk *negligée* and petticoat of brocaded lutestring for my dear Sally, with two dozen gloves, four bottles of lavender water, and two little reels.

The reels are to screw on the edge of the table, when she would wind silk or thread. The skein is to be put over them, and winds better than if held in two hands.

There is also a gimcrack corkscrew, which you must get some brother gimcrack to show you the use of. . . .

To Mary Stevenson Hewson

Preston, November 25 1771

Dear Friend: I thank you for your intelligence about my godson. I believe you are sincere, when you say you think him as fine a child as you wish to see. He had cut two teeth, and three, in another letter, make five; for I know you never write tautologies. If I have overreckoned, the number will be right by this time. His being like me in so many particulars pleases me prodigiously; and I am persuaded there is another, which you have omitted, though it must have occurred to you while you were putting them down. Pray let him have every thing he likes. I think it of great consequence while the features of the countenance are forming; it gives them a pleasant air, and, that being once become natural and fixed by habit, the face is ever after the handsomer for it, and on that much of a person's good fortune and success in life may depend. Had I been crossed as much in my infant liking and inclinations as you know I have been of late years, I should have been, I was going to say, not near so handsome; but as the vanity of that expression would offend other folks' vanity, I change it, out of regard to them, and say a great more homely. . . .

To Anthony Benezet*

London, August 22 1772

Dear Friend: I made a little extract from yours of April 27th of the number of slaves imported and perishing, with some close remarks on the hypocrisy of this country, which encourages such detestable commerce by laws for promoting the Guinea trade; while it piqued itself on its virtue, love of liberty, and the equity of its courts in setting free a single Negro. This was inserted in the *London Chronicle* of the 20th of June last.

I thank you for the Virginia address, which I shall also publish with some remarks. I am glad to hear that the disposition against keeping Negroes grows more general in North America. Several pieces have been lately printed here against the practice, and I hope in time it will be taken into consideration and suppressed by the legislature. Your labors have already been attended with great effects. I hope, therefore, you and your friends will be encouraged to proceed. My hearty wishes of success attend you.

---

* Anthony Benezet was a French-born philanthropist who spent most of his life in Philadelphia. He was a Quaker, and devoted most of his energies to improving the condition of the Negro and to polemicizing against the slave trade.

To Joseph Priestly

Dear Sir: I cannot, for want of sufficient premises, counsel you* *what* to determine; but if you please, I will tell you *how*. When those difficult cases occur, they are difficult chiefly because while we have them under consideration all the reasons *pro* and *con* are not present to the mind at the same time; but sometimes one set present themselves, and at other times another, the first being out of sight. Hence the various purposes or inclinations that alternately prevail and the uncertainty that perplexes us.

To get over this, my way is to divide half a sheet of paper by a line into two columns; writing over the one *pro* and over the other *con*; then during three or four days' consideration, I put down under the different heads short hints of the different motives that at different times occur to me, *for* or *against* the measure. When I have thus got them all together in one view, I endeavor to estimate their respective weights; and where I find two (one on each side) that seem equal, I strike them both out. If I find a reason *pro* equal to some *two* reasons *con,* I strike out the *three.* If I judge some *two* reasons *con* equal to some *three* reasons *pro,* I strike out the *five;* and thus proceeding I find at length where the balance lies; and if, after a day or two of farther consideration, nothing new that is of importance occurs on either side, I come to a determination accordingly. And though the weight of reasons cannot be taken with the precision of algebraic quantities, yet when each is thus considered separately and comparatively, and the whole lies before me, I think I can judge better and

* Joseph Priestly (1733–1804), eminent British chemist and divine, was engaged in examining the effect of different gases on the respiration of animals and plants. In 1767, he published a history of electricity, describing Franklin's work; in 1774, he discovered oxygen from mercuric oxide; in 1794, following Franklin's death, Priestly settled in Pennsylvania.

am less liable to make a rash step; and in fact have found great advantage from this kind of equation, in what may be called *moral* or *prudential algebra*.

To An Engraver in Paris*

Passy, June 24 1778

Sir: On reading again the prospectus and explanation of your intended print, I find the whole merit of giving freedom to America continues to be ascribed to me, which, as I told you in our first conversation, I could by no means approve of, as it would be unjust to the numbers of wise and brave men who, by their arms and counsels, have shared in the enterprise and contributed to its success (as far as it has yet succeeded) at the hazard of their lives and fortunes.

My proposition to you was, and continues to be, that instead of naming me in particular in the explanation of the print, it should be said: *"The Congress, represented by a senator in Roman dress, etc."* As it stands, I cannot consent to accept the honor you propose to do me by dedicating the print to me, which I understand is in this country considered as an approbation. And in my own country it would hurt my character and usefulness if I were to give the least countenance to such a pretension by recommending or proposing the sale of a print so explained. Upon these considerations I must request that, if you are determined to proceed in the engraving, you would in a new prospectus change the explanation as above proposed, and dedicate the print, not to me, but to the Congress.

---

* Antoine Borel, who had painted an allegorical picture showing Franklin in a toga with a wreath on his head, standing between America, supported by France, and America's enemies.

To Dr. Thomas Bond

Passy, March 16 1780

Dear Sir: I received your kind letter of September the 22nd, and I thank you for the pleasing account you give me of the health and welfare of my old friends, Hugh Roberts, Luke Morris, Philip Syng, Samuel Rhoads, etc., with the same of yourself and family. Shake the old ones by the hand for me, and give the young ones my blessing. For my own part, I do not find that I grow any older. Being arrived at seventy, and considering that by traveling farther in the same road I should probably be led to the grave, I stopped short, turned about, and walked back again; which having done these four years, you may now call me sixty-six. Advise those old friends of ours to follow my example; keep up your spirits, and that will keep up your bodies; you will no more stoop under the weight of age than if you had swallowed a handspike. . . .

To David Hartley*

Passy, December 15 1781

My Dear Friend: I received your favor of September 26th, containing your very judicious proposition of securing the spectators in the opera and play houses from the danger of fire. I communicated it where I thought it might be useful. You will see by the enclosed that the subject has been under consideration here. Your concern for the security of life, even the lives of your enemies, does honor to your heart and your humanity. But what are the lives of a few idle haunters of playhouses, compared with the many thousands of worthy men and honest industrious

* David Hartley was a Member of Parliament who opposed Britain's policy toward America and worked tirelessly for a reconciliation.

families butchered and destroyed by this devilish war? Oh that we could find some happy invention to stop the spreading of the flames, and put an end to so horrid a conflagration!

To Joseph Priestly

Passy, June 7 1782

Dear Sir: I should rejoice much if I could once more recover the leisure to search with you into the works of nature; I mean the *inanimate,* not the *animate* or moral part of them; the more I discovered of the former, the more I admired them; the more I know of the latter, the more I am disgusted with them. Men I find to be a sort of beings very badly constructed, as they are generally more easily provoked than reconciled, more disposed to do mischief to each other than to make reparation, much more easily deceived than undeceived, and having more pride and even pleasure in killing than in begetting one another; for without a blush they assemble in great armies at noonday to destroy, and when they have killed as many as they can, they exaggerate the number to augment the fancied glory; but they creep into corners or cover themselves with the darkness of night when they mean to beget, as being ashamed of a virtuous action. A virtuous action it would be, and a vicious one the killing of them, if the species were really worth producing or preserving; but of this I begin to doubt.

I know you have no such doubts, because in your zeal for their welfare you are taking a great deal of pains to save their souls. Perhaps as you grow older, you may look upon this as a hopeless project or an idle amusement, repent of having murdered in mephitic air so many honest, harmless mice, and wish that to prevent mischief you had used boys and girls instead of them. In what light we are viewed by superior beings may be gathered from a piece of late West India news which possibly has not yet reached you. A young angel of distinction being sent down to this world on some business for the first time, had an old courier-spirit assigned him as a guide. They arrived over the seas of Martinico, in the middle of the long day of obstinate fight between the fleets of Rodney and De Grasse. When, through the clouds of smoke, he saw the fire of the guns, the decks covered with mangled limbs and bodies dead or dying; the ships sinking, burning, or blown into the air; and the quantity of pain, misery and destruction, the crews yet alive were thus with so much eagerness dealing round to one another; he turned angrily to his guide, and said,

"You blundering blockhead, you are ignorant of your business; you undertook to conduct me to the earth, and you have brought me into hell!"

"No, Sir," says the guide, "I have made no mistake; this is really the earth, and these are men. Devils never treat one another in this cruel manner; they have more sense, and more of what men (vainly) call humanity."

But to be serious, my dear old friend, I love you as much as ever, and I love all the honest souls that meet at the London Coffee House. I only wonder how it happened that they and my older friends in England came to be such good creatures in the midst of so perverse a generation. I long to see them and you once more, and I labor for peace with more earnestness, that I may again be happy in your sweet society. . . .

To Sir Joseph Banks

Passy, July 27 1783

Dear Sir: I join with you most cordially in rejoicing at the return of peace. I hope it will be lasting, and that mankind will at length, as they call themselves reasonable creatures, have reason and sense enough to settle their differences without cutting throats; for, in my opinion, *there never was a good war, or a bad peace*. What vast additions to the conveniences and comforts of living might mankind have acquired, if the money spent in wars had been employed in works of public utility! What an extension of agriculture, even to the tops of our mountains; what rivers made navigable or joined by canals; what bridges, aqueducts, new roads, and other public works, edifices, and improvements, rendering England a complete paradise, might have been obtained by spending those millions in doing good which in the last war have been spent in doing mischief; in bringing misery into thousands of families, and destroying the lives of so many thousands of working people, who might have performed the useful labor!

I am pleased with the late astronomical discoveries made by our Society*. Furnished as all Europe now is with academies of science, with nice instruments and the spirit of experiment, the progress of human knowledge will be rapid, and discoveries made of which we have at present no conception. I begin to be almost sorry I was born so soon, since I cannot have the happiness of knowing what will be known one hundred years hence.

To Benjamin Webb

Passy, April 22 1784

Dear Sir: I received yours of the 15th instant, and the memorial it enclosed. The account they give of your situation grieves me. I send you herewith a bill for ten *louis d'ors*. I do not pretend to *give* such a sum; I only *lend* it to you. When you shall return to your country with a good character, you cannot fail of getting into some business, that will in time enable you to pay all your debts. In that case, when you meet with another honest man in similar

* The Royal Society of London, of which Banks was president

distress, you must pay me by lending this sum to him; enjoining him to discharge the debt by a like operation, when he shall be able, and shall meet with such another opportunity. I hope it may thus go through many hands, before it meets with a knave that will stop its progress. This is a trick of mine for doing a deal of good with a little money. I am not rich enough to afford *much* in good works, and so am obliged to be cunning and make the most of a *little*. . . .

To Samuel Mather

Passy, May 12 1784

Reverend Sir: You mention your being in your seventy-eighth year; I am in my seventy-ninth; we are grown old together. It is now more than sixty years since I left Boston, but I remember well both your father and grandfather*, having heard them both in the pulpit, and seen them in their houses. The last time I saw your father was in the beginning of 1724, when I visited him after my first trip to Pennsylvania. He received me in his library, and on my taking leave showed me a shorter way out of the house through a narrow passage, which was crossed by a beam over head. We were still talking as I withdrew, he accompanying me behind, and I turning partly towards him, when he said hastily, "*Stoop, stoop!*" I did not understand him, till I felt my head hit against the beam. He was a man that never missed any occasion of giving instruction, and upon this he said to me,

"*You are young, and have the world before you;* STOOP *as you go through it, and you will miss many hard thumps.*" This advice, thus beat into my head, has frequently been of use to me; and I often think of it, when I see pride

* Cotton and Increase Mather, influential ministers of Puritan Boston. They provided the theological justification for the Salem witchcraft trials of 1692.

mortified, and misfortunes brought upon people by their carrying their heads too high. . . .

To Thomas Percival

Passy, July 17 1784

Dear Sir: It is astonishing that the murderous practice of duelling, which you* so justly condemn, should continue so long in vogue. Formerly, when duels were used to determine lawsuits, from an opinion that Providence would in every instance favor truth and right with victory, they were excusable. At present, they decide nothing. A man says something, which another tells him is a lie. They fight, but whichever is killed, the point at dispute remains unsettled. To this purpose they have a pleasant little story here. A gentleman in a coffee house desired another to sit further from him.

"Why so?"

"Because, Sir, you stink."

"That is an affront, and you must fight me."

"I will fight you if you insist upon it, but I do not see how that will mend the matter. For if you kill me, I shall stink too; and if I kill you, you will stink, if possible, worse than you do at present."

How can such miserable sinners as we are entertain so much pride as to conceit that every offence against our imagined honor merits *death?* . . .

To William Franklin

Franklin's greatest personal tragedy was the fact that his son William, the governor of New Jersey, remained loyal

* Thomas Percival was an eminent British physician and writer on philosophical subjects.

to the Crown during the Revolution, and was an active leader of the American Loyalists. After the war he moved to London. Between 1776 and 1784 there was apparently no direct communication between father and son. William seems to have made the first move, and Franklin sent William's son Temple, whom he had educated since infancy and who served for many years as his secretary, to England with this letter.

Passy, August 16 1784

Dear Son: I received your letter of the 22nd ultimo, and am glad to find that you desire to revive the affectionate intercourse that formerly existed between us. It will be very agreeable to me; indeed nothing has ever hurt me so much and affected me with such keen sensations as to find myself deserted in my old age by my only son; and not only deserted, but to find him taking up arms against me in a cause wherein my good fame, fortune, and life were all at stake. You conceived, you say, that your duty to your King and regard for your country required this. I ought not to blame you for differing in sentiment with me in public affairs. We are men, all subject to errors. Our opinions are not in our own power; they are formed and governed much by circumstances that are often as inexplicable as they are irresistible. Your situation was such that few would have censured your remaining neuter, though there are natural duties which precede political ones and cannot be extinguished by them.

This is a disagreeable subject. I drop it. And we will endeavor, as you propose, mutually to forget what has happened relating to it, as well as we can. I send your son over to pay his duty to you. You will find him much improved. He is greatly esteemed and beloved in this country, and will make his way anywhere. . . .

I did intend returning this year; but the Congress, instead of giving me leave to do so, have sent me another commission which will keep me here at least a year longer;

and perhaps I may then be too old and feeble to bear the voyage. I am here among a people that love and respect me, a most amiable nation to live with; and perhaps I may conclude to die among them; for my friends in America are dying off, one after another, and I have been so long abroad that I should now be almost a stranger in my own country.

I shall be glad to see you when convenient, but would not have you come here at present. You may confide to your son the family affairs you wish to confer upon with me, for he is discreet; and I trust that you will prudently avoid introducing him to company that it may be improper for him to be seen with. . . .

To William Strahan

Passy, August 19 1784

Dear Friend: You* do not "approve the annihilation of profitable places, for you do not see why a statesman who does his business well should not be paid for his labor as well as any other workman." Agreed. But why more than any other workman? The less the salary the greater the honor. In so great a nation, there are many rich enough to afford giving their time to the public; and there are, I make no doubt, many wise and able men, who would take as much pleasure in governing for nothing, as they do in playing chess for nothing. It would be one of the noblest amusements. . . .

* William Strahan was printer to the King of England and a man of wealth and political influence.

To George Whatley*

My Dear Old Friend: I received your kind letter of May 3rd 1783. I am ashamed that it has been so long unanswered. The indolence of old age, frequent indisposition, and too much business are my only excuses. . . .

Your eyes must continue very good since you can write so small a hand without spectacles. I cannot distinguish a letter even of large print; but am happy in the invention of double spectacles which, serving for distant objects as well as near ones, make my eyes as useful to me as ever they were. If all the other defects and infirmities were as easily and cheaply remedied, it would be worth while for friends to live a good deal longer, but I look upon death to be as necessary to our constitution as sleep. We shall rise refreshed in the morning.

To George Whatley

Passy, May 23 1785

Dear Old Friend: I return your note of children received in the Foundling Hospital at Paris, from 1741 to 1755 inclusive, and I have added the years succeeding, down to 1770. Those since that period I have not been able to obtain. I have noted in the margin the gradual increase, *viz.* from every tenth child so thrown upon the public, till it comes to every third! Fifteen years have passed since the last account, and probably it may now amount to one half. Is it right to encourage this monstrous deficiency of natural affection? A surgeon I met with here excused the women of Paris, by saying, seriously, that they *could not* give suck;
    "*Car,*" said he, "*elles n'ont point de tetons.*"

* George Whatley, a London friend, was co-author with Franklin of a tract, *Principles of Trade*, published in London in 1774.

He assured me it was a fact, and bade me look at them, and observe how flat they were on the breast;

"They have nothing more there," said he, "than I have upon the back of my hand."

I have since thought that there might be some truth in his observation, and that possibly, nature finding they made no use of bubbies, has left off giving them any. Yet since Rousseau pleaded with admirable eloquence for the rights of children to their mother's milk, the mode has changed a little, and some ladies of quality now suckle their infants and find milk enough. May the mode descend to the lower ranks, till it becomes no longer the custom to pack their infants away, as soon as born, to the *Enfants Trouvés*, with the careless observation, that the King is better able to maintain them.

I am credibly informed that nine-tenths of them die there pretty soon, which is said to be a great relief to the institution, whose funds would not otherwise be sufficient to bring up the remainder. Except the few persons of quality above mentioned, and the multitude who send to the Hospital, the practice is to hire nurses in the country to carry out the children, and take care of them there. Here is an office for examining the health of nurses, and giving them licenses. They come to town on certain days of the week in companies to receive the children, and we often meet trains of them on the road returning to the neighboring villages, with each a child in her arms. But those, who are good enough to try this way of raising their children, are often not able to pay the expense; so that the prisons of Paris are crowded with wretched fathers and mothers confined *pour mois de nourrice**, though it is laudably a favorite charity to pay for them, and set such prisoners at liberty. I wish success to the new project of assisting the poor to keep their children at home, because I think there is no nurse like a mother (or not many), and that if parents

* For nurse's pay

did not immediately send their infants out of their sight they would in a few days begin to love them, and thence be spurred to greater industry for their maintenance. This is a subject you understand better than I, and, therefore, having perhaps said too much, I drop it. . . .

To Catherine Ray Greene

Philadelphia, March 2 1789

Dear Friend: Having now done with public affairs, which have hitherto taken up so much of my time, I shall endeavor to enjoy, during the small remainder of life that is left to me, some of the pleasures of conversing with my old friends by writing, since their distance prevents my hope of seeing them again. . . .

I received one of the bags of sweet corn you were so good as to send me a long time since, but the other never came to hand. Even the letter mentioning it, though dated December 10 1787, has been above a year on its way; for I received it but about two weeks since from Baltimore in Maryland. The corn I did receive was excellent, and gave me great pleasure. Accept my hearty thanks.

I am, as you suppose in the above-mentioned old letter, much pleased to hear that my young friend is "smart in the farming way," and makes such substantial fences. I think agriculture the most honorable of all employments . . . I congratulate your good spouse, that he, as well as myself, is now free from public cares, and that he can bend his whole attention to his farming, which will afford him both profit and pleasure; a business which nobody knows better how to manage with advantage.

I am too old to follow printing again myself, but, loving the business, I have brought up my grandson Benjamin to it, and have built and furnished a printing house for him, which he now manages under my eye. I have great pleasure in the rest of my grandchildren, who are now in number eight, and all promising, the youngest only six months old, but shows signs of great good nature. My friends here are numerous, and I enjoy as much of their conversation as I can reasonably wish; and I have as much health and cheerfulness as can well be expected at my age, now eighty-three. Hitherto this long life has been tolerably happy; so that, if I were allowed to live it over again, I should make no objection, only wishing for leave to do what authors do in a second edition of their works, correct some of my *errata*. Among the felicities of my life I reckon your friendship, which I shall remember with pleasure as long as that life lasts.

To David Hartley

Philadelphia, December 4 1789

M y Very Dear Friend: The convulsions in France* are attended with some disagreeable circumstances, but if by the struggle she obtains and secures for the nation its future liberty and a good constitution, a few years' enjoyment of those blessings will amply repay all the damages their acquisition may have occasioned. God grant that not only the love of liberty, but a thorough knowledge of the rights of man, may pervade all the nations of the earth, so that a philosopher may set his foot anywhere on its surface, and say, "This is my country." . . .

* The French Revolution had begun with the storming of the Bastille on July 14.

EPITAPH

The Body of
B Franklin Printer,
(Like the Cover of an Old Book
its Contents torn out
And stript of its Lettering & Gilding)
Lies here, Food for Worms.
But the Work shall not be lost;
For it will (as he believ'd) appear once more,
In a new and more elegant Edition
Revised and corrected
By the Author.

N. B. The Epitaph was composed in 1728 when Franklin was twenty-two years old. It does not appear on his tombstone. In the codicil to his will, written in 1789, Franklin asked that he be buried by the side of his wife and that a marble stone, "plain, with only a small moulding round the upper edge," inscribed with their names and the date, be placed over the grave. He died on April 17 1790.

Briefly,
ABOUT THE AUTHOR

During the eighty-four years of his lifetime
(1706 to 1790), Benjamin Franklin achieved
an extraordinary success in whatever he undertook. He was also one of the best beloved
persons in the world. Thomas Jefferson, who
succeeded him as Minister to France for the
young United States, believed him to be the
greatest American... He found "more respect and veneration attached to the character
of Dr. Franklin, in France, than to that of any
other person, foreign or native." A bright
light on the man, his time and his work
shines through his letters, writings and essays
which have been gathered for this book...
Hilda Lass, who edited our Franklin collection, is an American journalist. Formerly
employed on a New York news weekly, she
now works in Prague, where she lives with
her husband and their two sons. Her special
study of the Fabulous American dates back
to her years as a student at Vassar College.
The many-faceted genius of Benjamin Franklin has been of unflagging interest to her.